The Origins of the
Civilization of Angkor

DEBATES IN ARCHAEOLOGY

The Origins of the
Civilization of Angkor

Charles F. W. Higham

B L O O M S B U R Y
LONDON • NEW DELHI • NEW YORK • SYDNEY

Bloomsbury Academic
An imprint of Bloomsbury Publishing Plc

50 Bedford Square	175 Fifth Avenue
London	New York
WC1B 3DP	WC1B 3DP
UK	USA

www.bloomsbury.com

First published 2013

British Library Cataloguing-in-Publication Data
A catalogue record for this book is available from the British Library.

ISBN: HB: 9781780934198
ISBN: epub: 9781472502230
ISBN: epdf: 9781472502247

Library of Congress Cataloging-in-Publication Data
Higham, Charles, author.
The origins of the civilization of Angkor/Charles F.W. Higham.
pages cmIncludes bibliographical references and index.
Summary: "The book covers the background of environmental change,
the adoption of rice farming, archaeogenetics, the adoption of copper-based
metallurgy, the Iron Age and the origins of state formation" – Provided by publisher.
ISBN 978-1-7809-3419-8 (hardback : alk. paper) –
ISBN 978-1-4725-0223-0 (epub) – ISBN 978-1-4725-0224-7 (epdf)
1. Bronze age – Cambodia. 2. Iron age – Cambodia.
3. Antiquities, Prehistoric – Cambodia. 4. Antiquities,
Prehistoric – Southeast Asia. 5. Southeast Asia – Civilization.
6. Cambodia – Civilization. I. Title. GN778.32.C36H54
2013959.6'01 – dc23
2012045740

Typeset by Newgen Imaging Systems Pvt, Ltd., Chennai, India
Printed and bound in Great Britain

Contents

List of Figures

Acknowledgements

It was during a visit to the University of Pennsylvania in April, 2011 that the then director, Richard Hodges, invited me to write this book. I am most grateful to him for his encouragement. As in all my fieldwork and time spent in my study, I rely on the constant support of my wife Polly, for as if often noted, someone has to keep the home fires burning during extended periods of absence. Much of what I have written below has been assembled, pored over and synthesized over the course of fieldwork in Southeast Asia that now extends to 43 years. During much of that time, my Thai colleagues and co-directors during numerous excavations, Amphan Kijngam and Rachanie Thosarat, have made my participation not only possible, but also pleasurable.

I wish to acknowledge the kindness of Dr Berenice Bellina and Dr Warrachai Wiriyaromp for contributing illustrations to this volume, and to colleagues and students far too numerous to name, who have worked with me over the years. My son Thomas of the Oxford University Radiocarbon Dating Laboratory has enormously clarified the chronology presented below, through his insightful choice of dating materials, and the application of Bayesian statistics to the analysis of results.

My excavations have been funded by the Marsden Fund of New Zealand, Earthwatch and its Research Corps, the Ford Foundation, the British Academy, the University of Otago, the National Geographic Society and the Australian Research Council. I extend my thanks for their support.

1

The Debates

Towards the end of the sixteenth century, Portuguese missionaries began to explore the forested interior of Cambodia. It was here, that they encountered the abandoned complex known today as Angkor (Groslier 2005). Although some of the temples were still centres of Buddhist worship, most had been left to the encroaching jungle 150 years previously, when the court moved eastward to the vicinity of the modern capital, Phnom Penh. What they witnessed is best described in their own words. Antonio da Magdalena explored the ruins in 1586. 'The city', as he described it to the archivist Diogo do Couto, 'is square, with four principal gates, and a fifth, which serves the royal palace . . . the gates of each entrance are magnificently sculpted, so perfect, that they looked as if they were made from one stone'. He then commented on the fact that the stones had to be hauled to the city from a distance of 20 leagues, a feat that demanded a large and organized labour force. He then turned to the temple mausoleum of Angkor Wat, concluding that 'it is of such extraordinary construction that it is not possible to describe it with a pen, particularly since it is like no other building in the world. It has towers and decoration and all the refinements which human genius can conceive of'.

It was only a matter of years before we can read of the first speculation as to who might have been responsible for this abandoned city. In 1601, Marcello de Ribandeyra (1601) suggested that it was built by Alexander the Great, or the Romans. Forty-six years later, it was proposed that it was the work of the Roman Emperor Trajan.

The civilization of Angkor

The civilization with its capital at Angkor was one of several that flourished in Southeast Asia before the first European contact (Higham 2001). Angkor dominated the lowlands of Cambodia, and reached into adjacent parts of Thailand and Vietnam. In the former area, it bordered the civilization known as Dvaravati, which spread over the broad floodplain of the Chao Phraya River in Central Thailand, while the Cham kings ruled in the coastal plains of Central Vietnam. Debates on their origins have always incorporated one common theme: they display in their architecture, religion and language, pervasive influence from the civilizations of India. When translated, the inscriptions set up by Angkorian kings and grandees were found to be inscribed in Sanskrit as well as an archaic form of Khmer, the indigenous language of Cambodia. Sanskrit is the priestly language of the Hindu religion. Many Sanskrit words continue to be incorporated into Thai and Khmer. Thus the Thai province Chaiyaphum means victorious land. Simon de la Loubère was a French diplomat who visited the court of King Narai of Ayutthaya in Thailand in 1687. He noted that the language included words and expressions in Pali, another Indian language closely associated with Buddhism (Loubère 1693).

Many of the religious monuments of Angkor portray Hindu gods, such as Shiva and Vishnu, others are embellished with statues of the Buddha. The temples of Champa were usually dedicated to Shiva, while in Thailand, Buddhism was adopted by the rulers of Dvaravati. The temples themselves were often constructed, as in India, in brick, and the building designs owed much to Indian inspiration.

These facts gave rise to a simple explanation of origins, known as the process of Indianization. Expressed by the leading scholars of the day, it was formulated when serious archaeological research had barely begun, and our knowledge of the prehistoric inhabitants of Southeast Asia was in its infancy. A. Foucher (1922) proposed that Indian immigrants encountered 'savage populations of naked men'. Ramesh Majumdar (1944) wrote of Indian colonies in Southeast Asia, the only possible explanation for the saturation there of Indian customs and language. The Russian Leonid Sedov (1978) concluded that Indians 'acquainted the aborigines with various new techniques including methods of land reclamation, with handicrafts and the art of war'. George Cœdès was the doyen of Angkorian scholars, responsible for the translation of every known inscription from Sanskrit into French, and a man of unrivalled knowledge of the early states of Southeast Asia. In 1968 he wrote that Indianization involved a steady flow of immigrants who founded Indian kingdoms to a people 'still in the midst of late Neolithic civilization' (Cœdès 1968).

Cœdès and his French colleagues came to Southeast Asia in the wake of French colonial expansion into what are now Vietnam, Cambodia and Laos, and seeing the state of Angkor and its contemporaries as the result of a previous wave of colonization came easily to them. The decade of the 1960s, however, was a major turning point. By then, the French Eastern Empire was no more. Prehistorians were beginning to explore what had been widely regarded as a cultural backwater, and began to piece together what actually happened during the centuries before the foundation of local kingdoms. These findings in their turn, generated their own debates, particularly over chronology and the nature and the pace of cultural changes during the long duration of prehistory. Moreover, a new generation of historians began to explore the written records of Angkor, Champa and Dvaravati more deeply. Where Cœdès concentrated on the Sanskrit texts to reconstruct royal genealogies, Vickery (1998) incorporated the old Khmer record to peel off the veneer of Indianization and reveal a deep legacy of indigenous gods, names and customs.

Four debates

The rulers of Southeast Asian kingdoms were sustained by the surpluses generated by those who toiled in the heat of the day to cultivate rice. Without rice, it is hard to envisage how the court societies, with their ostentatious temples, bureaucrats, scribes, architects and craft specialists could have been. Rice is a remarkable plant. It is essentially a marsh grass, that can flourish even on poor soils with no fallow season, provided that there is sufficient rainfall. It is therefore inevitable, that the first debate to be considered is why and how, after at least 50,000 years of hunting and gathering in the heat of Southeast Asia, should some communities begin to cultivate rice, and herd domestic animals. Let us contrast this situation with what happened to the southeast, in Australia. Both areas were occupied by anatomically modern humans who left their African homeland by 60,000 years ago. By following a line of least resistance, the warm coastal tracts of India and Southeast Asia, these hunter-gatherers ultimately crossed by boat into Australia. In the fullness of time, agriculture and stock raising were adopted on the Asian mainland, to be followed by the foundation of early states. But in Australia, hunting and gathering continued down to and beyond the period of European settlement. Who was responsible for this transition to farming, the so-called Neolithic Revolution? When did it take place, and what was its impact on human behaviour?

The second debate revolves round the timing and the impact of metallurgy. In Southeast Asia, this involved the smelting of copper and tin ores, and mixing the metals together to form bronze. Although the presence of a discrete Bronze Age was first identified in the 1870s when the Cambodian site of Samrong Sen was excavated (Mansuy 1902), the excavations at two sites in Northeast Thailand a century later generated a blaze of controversy when it was claimed that the prehistoric inhabitants of Non Nok Tha and Ban Chiang were responsible for the earliest bronzes in the world (Solheim 1968, Gorman and Charoenwongsa 1975). Widespread interest among archaeologists reflected the significance of metallurgy as a catalyst for cultural change. Essentially, bronzes by their very nature called on a high degree of labour to secure the raw materials, and expertise to alloy and cast the molten metal. The ownership of bronze weapons and ornaments was a ready means to advertise social standing and prestige. The greater their rarity, the more desirable bronzes would become. In the Near East, the Indus Valley and in China, it is possible to link the rise of social elites with increasingly elaborate bronzes. But in Southeast Asia until very recently, no such development has been identified. This particular debate therefore, revolves round identifying when metallurgy was adopted, where the knowledge came from, and its actual impact on the lives of those who were involved.

If bronze had transformational potential for human societies, iron had even more. Iron ore in Southeast Asia is more widely available than the ores of copper or tin, but it also requires greater heat to extract metal. Once achieved however, the smiths forged ornaments, weapons and tools used in manufacturing or agriculture. So we turn to a further debate: when did iron become part of the technological repertoire of prehistoric people in Southeast Asia, and how can we measure its impact on social change?

The last debate is the most complex, for it involves one of the most significant developments in the history of our species: the origins of civilization. Archaeologists can recognize an extinct civilization through its hardware in the form of large and impressive buildings, often concentrated into what we term a city. Such buildings in effect represent frozen energy, and reflect an intensive organization of labour.

The hardware often includes massive tombs and temples, representing both the status of the ruling elite, and the ideology that sustained them. Recording events, payments, predictions for the future, claims to special powers through a system of writing are also widespread in early states. It is from such evidence that we can also attempt to isolate and understand the software in the transition to the state. How does an elite, representing a tiny fraction of the population, come to hold sway over the majority? Under what sanctions, or circumstances, do those who toil in the rice fields give up a surplus of what they produce to sustain their rulers? Can we identify any changing circumstances that could have encouraged the formation of a ruling dynasty able to occupy a palace, hold sway over a large population of followers and appropriate to itself wealth and exceptional status? Such circumstances might have involved, for example, a growing population, the need to respond to external military pressure, the possibility of controlling new trading opportunities or ownership of a vital resource, such as salt, or iron ore. In Southeast Asia, there is no final resolution to this fascinating question, but we are much closer to understanding what happened than when it was assumed that the arrival of sophisticated Indian colonists tutored a simple indigenous population into the arts of a civilized life.

2

Southeast Asia in 2000 BC

Four thousand years ago, those living in Southeast Asia (Figure 2.1) inherited a land drastically changed from that of their ancestors over the previous ten millennia, and their descendants were to experience just as profound changes, but of a different kind. With the end of the last ice age, about 12,000 years ago, the sea level progressively rose by at least 120 metres. In Southeast Asia, this resulted in the loss of land the size of India, and the creation of many islands which had formerly been relatively high ground. By 2000 BC, the sea actually rose about 2 metres higher than its present level, and formed a new shoreline that is now stranded, many kilometres inland. The area lost to the sea, known as Sundaland, would have been home to many groups of hunter-gatherers whose ancestors, Anatomically Modern Humans, had spread into Southeast Asia and beyond in Australia at least 50,000 years ago from their African homeland. Over this vast expanse of time, these hunter-gatherers adapted to a range of different environments. Naturally, nothing is known of those who lived where the sea has now encroached, but we can illuminate the rhythm of life of their descendants, who lived along the old, raised shorelines.

One such site is known as Nong Nor. It is situated today about 22 kilometres from the Gulf of Siam, covered by modern rice fields (Higham and Thosarat 1998). Excavations revealed occupation by coastal hunter-gatherers who had lived there, briefly, in about 2400 BC. They chose to live on what was then a low promontory overlooking

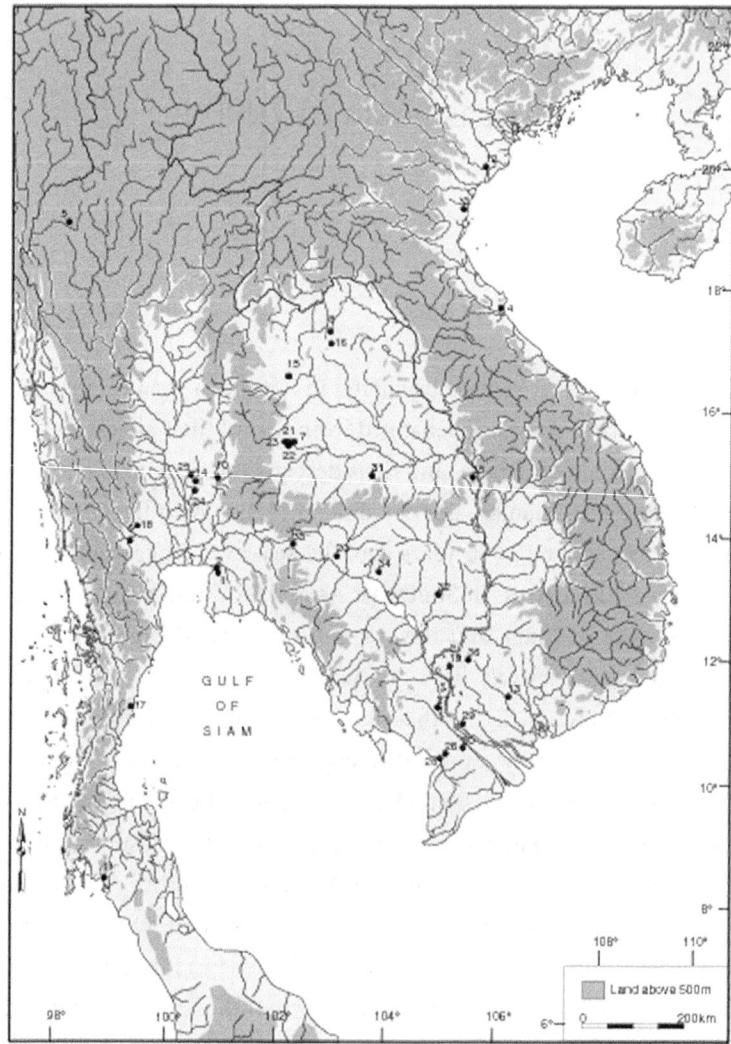

Figure 2.1 Map of the sites mentioned in the text. Nong Nor, 2. Khok Phanom Di, 3. Quynh Van, 4. Bau Tro, 5. Spirit Cave, 6. Khok Phanom Di, 7. Ban Non Wat, 8. Ban Chiang, 9. Ban Kao, 10. Khok Charoen, 11. Moh Khiew, 12. Man Bac, 13. An Son, 14. Non Pa Wai, 15. Non Nok Tha, 16. Ban Na Di, 17. Khao Sam Kaeo, 18. Ban Don Ta Phet, 19. Prohear, 20. Phum Snay, 21. Noen U-Loke, 22. Non Muang Kao, 23. Non Ban Jak, 24. Tha Kae, 25. Phu Noi, 26. Oc Eo, 27. Angkor Borei, 28. Nen Chua, 29. Go Thap, 30. Go Xoai, 31. Phum Phon, 32. Ishanapura, 33. Sdok Kak Thom, 34. Angkor, 35. Wat Phu, 36. Banteay Prei Nokor.

a large marine embayment, sheltered from the open sea to which access was gained by means of an inlet about 5 km to the north. Several other similar sites were also found round this embayment. The hunter-gatherers collected cockle shells from the sandy beaches in their thousands, and these accumulated into thick middens. But examination of the midden contents also revealed how they had gone out into the open sea to fish for bull sharks and eagle rays, and hunted seals. No evidence was found for the consumption of rice, and there were no domestic animal bones. However, they made pottery vessels, and ground and polished their axes. One burial was found, an old woman, interred in a seated, crouched position under several pottery vessels. Clearly, these people inherited a long tradition of adaptation to a marine environment, and could stay in the same settlement for long enough to feel a need to fashion and fire pottery vessels, for if a group is regularly moving from place to place, a pottery vessel being fragile, has little value.

As the sea level retreated, so Nong Nor ceased to be attractive for those long accustomed to life on or near the shore. Four centuries later, in about 2000 BC, we can track down a second hunter-gatherer community just 14 km to the north, at a site called Khok Phanom Di (Higham and Thosarat 2004). This was altogether a different settlement to Nong Nor. Critically, it was located at the mouth of the estuary of the Bang Pakong River. A mangrove-fringed estuary is one of the richest habitats known, in terms of natural abundance of food and energy. This is firmly based on the fact that mangroves continuously shed their leaves, thus providing the basis for a food chain that begins with small marine organisms, and proceeds through their predators, to the small fish, crabs and shellfish, thence to larger fish and ultimately, to human communities. Moreover, estuaries seasonally attract large shoals of breeding fish while the rivers and open sea offer further opportunities for fishing and easy access to exchange routes. All these advantages encourage permanent settlement rather than the mobility so often associated with hunter-gatherer communities. There were doubtless disadvantages, not least the swarms of malarial mosquitoes which one associates with such habitats. However, deep in the lowest occupation layers at Khok Phanom Di, we can reconstruct many aspects of the life of a maritime hunter-gatherer society.

A direct link is found between the first people to occupy the site and those of Nong Nor, through their very similar styles of pottery vessels and bone fishhooks, awls and points. Both groups also fashioned highly polished stone adzes, made from stone that had to be imported. At Khok Phanom Di, caches of such adzes were found, together with the clay anvils and burnishing stones that were used first to form and then to polish their pottery vessels. The mound rapidly rose in height as shellfish were brought to the site, and then dumped into middens. *Anadara granosa* was the dominant species, a bivalve adapted to the sandy beaches that must have stretched out to sea at low tide. These middens also contain the remains of a variety of fish, and crabs. What we don't find in the early levels, are any signs of domestic animals. There are no dog bones, nor any sign of pigs or cattle. Nor is there any evidence for the cultivation of rice, although some fragments of rice chaff were present as temper in exotic potsherds (Vincent 2004). There were also a few indications of rice in the occupation layers, but it is held unlikely that it was locally cultivated, since rice is not adapted to salty conditions.

Treatment of the dead is a key to unlock social aspects of an extinct society. The earliest occupants of Khok Phanom Di buried the dead in shallow graves, within their middens. A child was found interred in a foetal, crouched position, while two men and a woman were placed extended, on their backs with the head directed to the east, one accompanied by a handful of shell beads. Two of the adults and the child exhibited bone conditions that suggested that they suffered from a blood disorder that, while shielding the individual from malaria, caused anaemia. This genetic disorder may well reflect many generations of survival in a malarial environment (Tayles 1999).

If Khok Phanom Di had been abandoned after this initial occupation phase, it would have closely resembled what was found at Nong Nor. However, the favourable estuarine conditions enabled this society to continue living there for a further four centuries, and as the mound rapidly accumulated, so we can reconstruct its progression through time against a backdrop of changes in the physical and social environment. This sequence is divided into seven mortuary phases. The second of these reveals a marked change in the treatment of the dead. They were now interred in tight clusters, laid out on a chequer-board pattern, still with the head to the east. In some cases, mineralized wood under the skeleton suggested that they were placed on a bier, and to add to the increasingly complex rituals that attended funerals, bodies were sprinkled with red ochre and wrapped in a shroud of asbestos sheets. Mortuary offerings now included brilliantly polished and decorated pottery vessels. One man stood out for his lavish ornaments that included 39,000 shell beads. Cowrie shells were also found as mortuary offerings, as well as a rhinoceros tooth and bangles fashioned from fish vertebrae. The layout of the burial clusters was complemented by a thick shell midden that ran between them, and even turned at right angles, as if it had accumulated against a structure of some sort. This, combined with the presence of the holes that would once have held the upright posts of a building, strongly suggests that there had once been mortuary buildings to contain the dead.

The study of the bones themselves reveals a very high proportion of newly born infants. The adults, many of which continued to exhibit symptoms of anaemia, had well-developed bones with robust musculature, which Tayles (1999) has suggested might have been the result of such activities as paddling canoes, or kneading and converting clay into pottery vessels.

The third mortuary phase continued in the established tradition of interment in tight groups lying over the ancestors, associated with finely made pottery vessels and shell jewellery (Figure 2.2). Half of

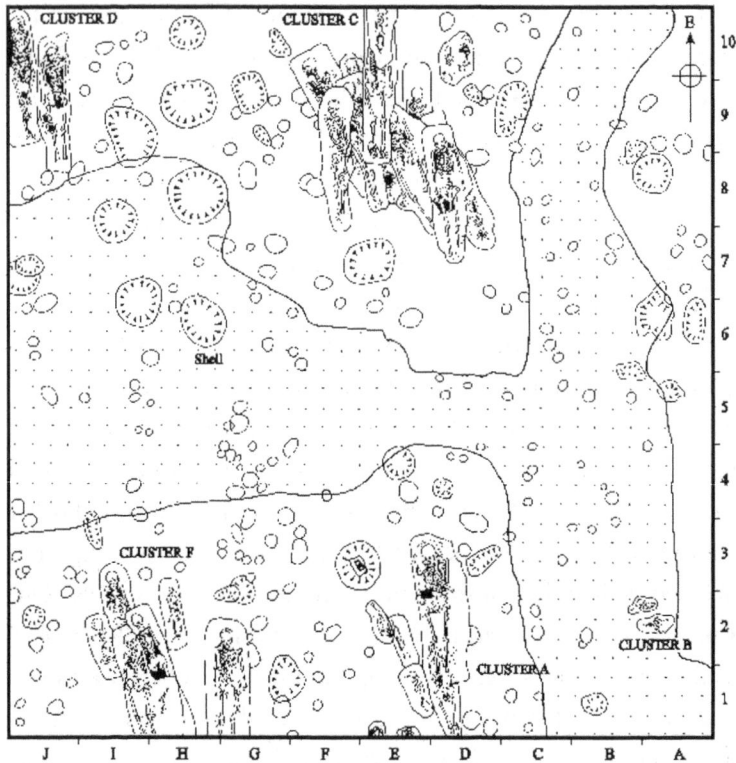

Figure 2.2 Plan of the mortuary phase 3 cemetery at Khok Phanom Di.

all graves also continued to contain newly born infants. However, during the course of this phase, there were also a series of important changes. The most significant of these comes from the study of isotopes in the human teeth (Bentley et al. 2007), which show that some women interred at Khok Phanom Di were raised in a different environment, and must thus have come to the site from elsewhere. It was at this juncture, that people began to fashion large hoes made from granite, and convert shells into knives. An examination of the wear patterns on these knives suggests that they were used as sickles to harvest a grass, such as rice (Higham 1993). Significantly, it was also now that shellfish adapted to the landward edge of mangroves began to increase in relative frequency, and we find that the bones of freshwater crabs and fish were more abundant. All these leads suggest that the newcomers might have brought with them, the knowledge and practice of cultivating rice, but the clinching evidence for this comes from a certain source: the actual remains of partially digested food found in a woman's pelvic area.

The survival of organic remains at Khok Phanom Di was exceptional, and included the remains of what might well have been this woman's last meal. It included a mass of small fish bones and scales, as well as fragments of rice chaff. A second grave contained the remains of faeces, and again, rice was found which revealed the features of a domesticated variety (Thompson 1996). There were also mouse hairs, and the remains of a beetle adapted to living in rice stores. It seems highly likely that the rice this person consumed had been stored in an environment that harboured mice and beetles. This major new development at Khok Phanom Di took place as far as the radiocarbon determination reveals, in about 1600–1700 BC. It also sparks a debate: was rice domesticated initially at Khok Phanom Di and similar coastal sites, or was it introduced from elsewhere?

Before turning to this issue, we can track through the sequel at Khok Phanom Di before the site was abandoned, probably in about 1500–1400 BC. During Mortuary Phase 4, the freshwater indicators continued, and shell reaping knives were still made. There was a marked drop in infant mortality, but four of the five children encountered had suffered from severe anaemia. Men were physically less robust than their predecessors, and they were increasingly distinguished from women when interred: men were found with large, fractured ornaments fashioned from turtle carapaces, whereas women were accompanied by the anvils and burnishing stones used to manufacture and decorate pottery vessels. But this was to change for the sea level rose again with Mortuary Phase 5, and the shell sickles and granite hoes ceased to be found. There was a reversion to marine hunting and gathering, and at the same time, a profound change in the rituals of death. In place of the traditional groups, we find a single grave far larger than was necessary to contain the body of the woman within it. She had been interred in upper garments embellished with over 120,000 shell beads. There were shell discs on her chest, shell ear ornaments and a shell bangle. Her body had been covered in red ochre, and lay under a pyramid of clay cylinders destined to be converted into pottery vessels. Several completed vessels, each a masterpiece, were laid beside her, and by her right ankle, there was a potter's anvil and a shell containing two well-used burnishing stones (Figure 2.3). This staggering mortuary wealth was matched by that associated with an infant, not yet 2 years old at death, in an adjacent grave. Again, there were clay cylinders heaped over the body thousands of shell beads, a shell bangle, fine pots, but also a miniature clay anvil placed beside the infant's right ankle. It is

Figure 2.3 Burial 15 at Khok Phanom Di, a woman interred with over 120,000 shell beads, discs, a bangle and outstanding pottery vessels. A clay anvil and two burnishing stones lay beside her ankles.

hard not to identify this woman as a master potter, particularly given the strong musculature of her wrists, and the infant as her daughter, a future potter who suffered a premature death. Her wealth might well have been due to her expertise in manufacturing vessels for exchange that brought to the site, exotic shell from a coralline environment. Although the absolute amount of wealth fell back with the ensuing phase 6, rituals were still intense, for two women and a child were found buried within a raised mortuary chamber of clay wall foundations and a clay floor. They wore thousands of shell beads and again, were accompanied by their clay anvils. In front of them, however, enclosed within a wooden building, was a row of graves containing men and women, as well as newly born probable twins, with much more modest offerings (Figure 2.4). A lively discussion could be generated from this information, as to whether this hunter-gatherer society was now divided into rich and poor social groups. However, after a handful of scattered burials representing mortuary phase 7, the sequence spanning perhaps as many as 20 generations came to an end.

Although no other Southeast Asian site has provided comparably detailed information on adaptation to a marine environment, there is no doubt, following the inundation of Sundaland, that extensive tracts of coast attracted human settlement. Thus there are many sites on the raised beaches of Vietnam that recall what was found at Khok Phanom Di. Probably dating between 3000–2500 BC, the site of Bau Du contained superimposed shell middens in which the remains of crabs, fish and turtles are abundant (Ha Van Tan 1997). Quynh Van is a settlement 6 metres thick in which 31 flexed inhumation burials were recovered, and where pottery and polished stone tools were manufactured. Bau Tro revealed on excavation, three periods when shell middens were deposited between 2500–2000 BC. The Vietnamese archaeologists traditionally label these prehistoric groups 'Neolithic' because of the presence of pottery and polished stone tools. However, this term is reserved by many specialists to those communities

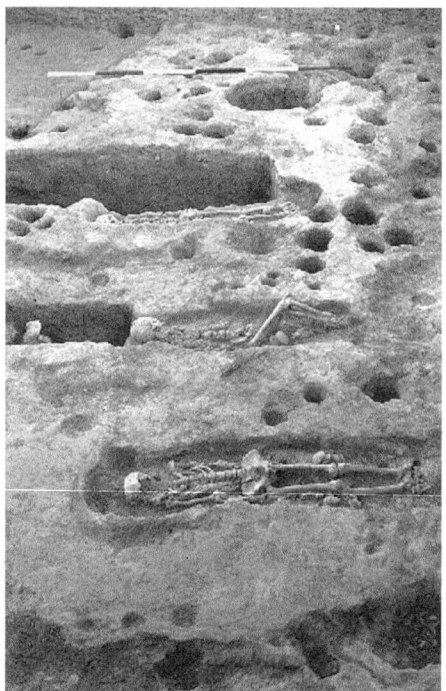

Figure 2.4 During mortuary phase 6 at Khok Phanom Di, a row of graves was laid out in front of a raised clay platform which itself contained a mortuary chamber.

engaged in food production rather than hunting and gathering. No convincing evidence has yet been published from Vietnam to show that these coastal groups were involved in cultivating rice or millet, or maintaining domestic animals.

The descendants of the maritime hunter-gatherers of Sundaland were able to continue enjoying the natural plenty provided by the estuaries and the coasts of Southeast Asia formed when the sea rose higher than its present position. There is no reason why relatively sedentary hunter-gatherers should not make pottery vessels, or polish their stone tools, and the evidence from Khok Phanom Di reveals the development of considerable social complexity. The inland plains and uplands, however, present a sharp contrast. In the latter habitat, the vast majority of prehistoric sites comprise caves or rock shelters, where the remains of transient occupation are both preserved, and relatively easily identified. Here, we can learn a lesson from the few bands of hunter-gatherers who survive in Trang Province, southern Thailand, where the Mani continue in their traditional ways. They prefer to live in the forest, foraging and gathering, during the dry season, but take shelter in caves with the onset of the rains. During the former, a social group of less than 20 individuals make temporary shelters of bamboo, leaves and tree bark, and hunt for macaques, gibbons and squirrels of the forest, or collect shellfish and trap fish. Their ephemeral habitations would leave little trace in the archaeological record, whereas the caves, particularly when hearths were used to cook their food, would be more prone to survive.

What we find then, is that over a period of at least 30,000 years, such small social groups maintained themselves in the forested interior uplands, engaged in what we might term broad spectrum foraging. The animal bones include a wide range of mammals, from the wild water buffalo and cattle, down to the tiniest squirrels and deer. Plant remains likewise reflect many uses, from stimulants, poisons to tip their arrowheads, oil for lighting and of course, a range of edible items. These groups have several titles. The most widespread is Hoabinhian, a label taken from the Vietnamese province where the first cave sites were examined in the 1920s (Colani 1927). There are many cave sites in the hills of northern Thailand and thence south into Kanchanaburi and the Peninsula. One of these sites, known as Spirit Cave, is located on a steep slope overlooking the Khong Stream in northern Thailand. Excavations there in the 1960s by Chester Gorman employed fine mesh screening of the cultural deposits, which yielded the remains of 22 plant genera. Moreover, a few potsherds were embedded into the surface of layer 2. A second site, Banyan Valley Cave, also contained potsherds and a few rice husks. These finds encouraged Solheim (1972) to conclude that this remote, forested region witnessed the transition into plant domestication at a very early date indeed. However, first the rice was found to come from a local wild variety, and more recently, the resin that coated one of the potsherds has been radiocarbon dated to the second millennium BC, far too late to be relevant to the quest to identify an origin of rice domestication. Rather, this and related sites point to a long-term and stable adaptation to the forested uplands.

Southeast Asia contains many broad riverine plains, particularly in Central Thailand, Cambodia and the Khorat Plateau of northeast Thailand. These could well have supported a large population of hunter-gatherers, given the plentiful sources of fish, shellfish and mammals. Indeed, there were until quite recently, herds of three species of wild cattle, as well as large and small deer, wild pigs, elephants and rhinoceros. However, deforestation and population growth have conspired to exterminate these animals from much of the region, and the erosion and the reworking of the landscape that has followed, will have covered early prehistoric sites making them hard if not impossible to find. Therefore our knowledge of human settlement at 2000 BC in the inland plains is a virtual blank. However, by venturing north into Guangxi Province of China, some idea of the sort of settlement that there might have been is readily apparent.

Open sites normally close to or adjacent to rivers have been excavated at Gexinqiao, Baida and Kantun. Dating between 7000–3000 BC, they contain many flaked stone tools, including choppers, points and scrapers, as well as polished stone adzes. Two tightly flexed human burials were found at Gexinqiao, associated with nothing other than river cobbles, although some cord-marked potsherds were found (Xie et al. 2003). Very extensive excavations at Beidaling, covering 1,600 m², again yielded stone tools in all stages of manufacture, as well as some polished adzes and a scatter of potsherds. Eight graves were also uncovered. At Chongtang, in southern Guangxi province, a veritable cemetery of at least 26 graves has been identified and clearly there were extensive exchange links with coastal communities, for some cowrie shells have been recovered there (He and Chen 2008). The point about this site is that clearly, there were large hunter-gatherer sites in the inland plains of southern China that were occupied, or visited often enough to lead to the formation of cemeteries to contain the dead. The principal activity was the manufacture of stone tools, and the inhabitants were able to produce ceramic vessels. While no such sites have been opened in the inland plains of Thailand, Cambodia or Vietnam, the presence of flexed burials in some later Neolithic sites, such as Ban Non Wat, strongly suggests that hunter-gatherers did live in such habitats (Figure 2.5).

We must now confront a major issue: where were the origins of rice domestication? It is impossible to underestimate the importance of this plant in the history of Southeast Asia. In lowland riverine and coastal plains of Southeast Asia today, rice fields literally stretch to

Figure 2.5 Two flexed burials at Ban Non Wat were interred with bivalve shells, a pot, and most unusual shell beads. They were probably hunter-gatherers.

the horizon. Where there is sufficient water, two or even three crops can be harvested annually. Several proposals have been advanced which attempt to identify and explain why hunter-gatherers, who had been adapting to a range of environments, as we have seen, for tens of thousands of years, should so radically change their subsistence to include the cultivation of this plant. Even during the height of the last glacial, Southeast Asia remained relatively warm and inviting to human settlement. The major crisis affecting the area when the ice age ended, was a sharply rising sea level loss of low-lying land. This would have necessitated many communities to adapt and move, but paradoxically the rising sea actually formed a longer shoreline, and this was settled by marine hunter-gatherers who showed no interest in experimenting with plant domestication.

There are still two alternative models that could explain where and when food producing replaced hunting and gathering. The first would involve a local origin within Southeast Asia, and the second the expansion into the region of farming group from outside. There are several sources of information that bear on these two possibilities. The first calls on traditional archaeological reasoning. Virtually all societies past or present, have a mental template of what design a house should take, what clothes are appropriate, the preferred form of their pottery vessels and how they should be embellished by decoration, and how they dispose of the dead. Therefore, if a social group resolved to move its settlement to a new location, it is reasonable to expect that its members will take with them these preferences. Let us say, therefore, that two prehistoric settlements in Southeast Asia separated by several hundred kilometres exhibit close similarities in their material culture and their subsistence economy, it is reasonable to link them genetically into one larger grouping.

People also take with them their genes and their language when they move. Increasingly, it is possible to trace the passage of prehistoric human expansion by the analysis of genetic variation in their descendants, and if it survives, the ancient DNA in those who were actually involved. Thus, a shared genetic mutation is a sure sign that those sharing it, are related. Nor is this restricted to human genes. If a group brought with them their rice, dogs or pigs, or if rats hitchhiked in their boats, then the DNA of these plants and animals is also a fruitful source of information. Languages may also hold a key to unlocking past expansions. Of course, new languages can be learned, and some can become extinct. But shared words, language structures, and innovations remain a valid approach to identifying what happened in prehistory.

What, then, do these approaches when combined, tell us about the origins of rice cultivation in Southeast Asia or beyond? The answer regarding indigenous origins is, virtually nothing. In 1976, Chester Gorman and I concocted a possible model for testing. We suggested that the piedmont area, between the uplands of the Phetchabun Mountains and the flat Khorat Plateau, might be a candidate for this transition. We imagined that the marshes formed where rivers debouched from the uplands, and where wild rice could well have flourished, would be a location where hunter-gatherers might have developed an interest in propagating rice to expand a natural harvest. A graduate student was given the opportunity to explore and test this model, but found no prehistoric sites that could have borne witness to such a transition. The closest anyone has come to supporting early agriculture comes not from archaeology, but from palynology, the study of pollen. Lake Kumphwapi is a large body of water located in the northern part of the Khorat Plateau, about 30 km southwest of the prehistoric site of Ban Chiang. Cores taken through the lake sediments have identified not only a sharp rise in the quantity of charcoal fragments, but also a decline in some local species of tree pollen. Radiocarbon determinations from above and below this horizon indicate that deforestation burning took place during the fifth millennium BC. White (1997) has suggested that this event, which took place with little if any preceding evidence for forest clearance, could reflect an expansionary movement of farmers from southwestern China at least two millennia before there is any actual archaeological evidence for a settlement site. Indeed, in 1982, I was involved in an intensive site survey on the Lake Kumphawapi floodplain, and found no evidence for Neolithic settlement at such an early date. It must also be stressed that hunter-gatherers are prone to setting fire to the forest, for this brings light and sun to the deforested area and in freshening grass growth with the rainy season, attracts wild deer and cattle. At Khok Phanom Di, we found similar evidence for burning episodes in our pollen cores antedating the settlement of this site, but concluded that these could have been generated by the local hunter-gatherers, or even lightning strikes that often set trees on fire when the monsoon storms follow the long dry season.

Any debate on the origins of the Southeast Asian Neolithic needs to identify where rice cultivation and animal husbandry first took hold. Recent excavations in China, particularly those where flotation of archaeological deposits has led to the recovery of rice remains, have narrowed our search to the wetlands of the Yangtze River and coastal plains found north and south of that great river's estuary. Recovering prehistoric rice is essential to any understanding of two relevant processes. The first is cultivation, that is human intervention in the growth patterns of wild rice, such as harvesting the grain with a sickle, or removing the plant's natural competitors by weeding or eliminating vermin. The second is domestication, by which is meant the adaptations in the plant morphology stimulated by cultivation. One of these, and a key to the success of early cultivators, is selection for non-shattering plants. When rice matures, the natural procedure is for the seed to disperse by breaking its bond with the plant at the spikelet base. If one takes a sickle to a stand of ripened wild rice, much will be lost when shattering takes place. But in the event of a genetic mutation in favour of a strong link between the grain and the spikelet, more rice will be retained and harvested. In other words, what is bad for the plant is good for the harvester.

Fortunately, spikelet bases often survive in archaeological contexts where the actual grain does not, because it was consumed. Moreover, its morphology reflects whether or not domestication was under way. Thompson (1996) used the shape of the spikelet bases at Khok Phanom Di to identify domestic rice. Following intensive excavations involving flotation at the Chinese site of Tianluoshan, it is possible to follow and date the course of domestication there (Fuller et al. 2010). There are other indicators of domestication, such as grain size and a more erect plant less prone to branching laterally, and all contribute to deciphering the central issue: when and where did domestic rice become a dominant part of subsistence. The answer is now emerging. Rice was part of the diet at Shang Shan in the Lower Yangtze area between 10,000–8000 BC, but there is no evidence that it was not wild. Again in the Central Yangtze margins of Lake Dongting, much rice was recovered from Pengtoushan and Bashidang between 8000–6000 BC but again, without strong evidence for domestication. However, domestic rice remains have been found at the lower Yangtze site of Kuhaoqiao between 6000–5400 BC. The best evidence thereafter in this same region comes from Tianluoshan.

Tianluoshan was located in a marshy lowland environment, and has been excavated over a very large area. This has revealed the wooden foundations for domestic structures, the remains of a boat, paddles and even a footbridge over a prehistoric river. Anaerobic conditions have preserved biological remains; there are many bone and wooden artefacts, including the shoulder blades of cattle converted into hoes or spades. Living surfaces still contain caches of acorns, and the fine screening of cultural deposits has yielded a large sample of rice spikelet bases. These indicate that by about 4900 BC, a minority were showing signs of domesticity, and that over the ensuing centuries, this proportion steadily increased. It is also important to note that rice was but one component of a varied diet that included many other water plants, as well as both wild and domestic animals. It was only with the later Liangzhu culture of this region in the late fourth millennium BC that domestic rice became a significant, even a dominant, part of the economy.

Fuller et al. (2010) having established that japonica rice came under cultivation, and in due course domestication in the lower Yangtze Valley region, then identified a series of thrusts outward on the basis of rice remains found beyond this centre of origin. One of these, thrust number 5, involved movement into Southeast Asia. Another saw the expansion of rice farming up the Yangtze River into Yunnan and Sichuan provinces. Others involved northern China, Korea and Japan, while it is also evident that rice farmers crossed into Taiwan. In Central Thailand, there is also evidence for the introduction of domestic millet, with an ultimate origin in northern China.

The next stage in our enquiry is to investigate the archaeological, linguistic and genetic evidence for this proposed thrust, for testing a model is an essential procedure to confirm, negate or refine it. Archaeologically, there is a sharp distinction in Southeast Asia between the hunter-gatherer settlements described above, and lowland settlements that are characterized by an entirely new range of artefact types and mortuary behaviour. The first of these to be uncovered in detail is known as Ban Kao, in Kanchanaburi Province, soon to be followed by Khok Charoen, 220 km to the northeast, in the valley of the Pasak River (Sørensen and Hatting 1967, Ho 1984). Excavations at Ban Kao uncovered a cemetery in which the dead were laid out on their backs, with a consistent set of grave offerings centring on pottery vessels, bones from domestic pigs and polished stone adzes, but also including shell jewellery. The site has also yielded clay spindle whorls. As early as 1963, Sørensen (1963) suggested that the form of the pottery vessels presented close parallels with those recovered from Chinese sites, and suggested that there had been an expansionary movement to Ban Kao and related sites. At the time, such migration theories were unfashionable and the idea generated little if any enthusiasm from members of a small band of colleagues. However, progressively his prescience has been confirmed, as more sites have been excavated. These have closely similar features to Ban Kao: a similar mortuary ritual, the presence of domestic animal bones, evidence from the spindle whorls of a weaving industry and perhaps most significant, a preferred style for decorating pottery vessels. There is virtually an infinite choice in choosing the shape of a clay pot, and how to decorate it. Once fired, the vessel either complete or in fragments, will survive for millennia. A recurring feature of the pots in question is a particular style of decoration that involved incising designs comprising parallel lines, infilled with impressions and sometimes with paint. This is known as the incised and impressed (I&I) style. I&I vessels are known from sites in Central and Northeast Thailand, Cambodia and Vietnam from the north to south. The basic similarity in style and motif argues in favour of a common origin. This possibility has been pursued by Fiorella Rispoli from Southeast Asia northward, and she has been able to trace its origins in earlier sites in China (Rispoli 2008). Zhang and Hung (2010) have done likewise, their starting point being China, before pursuing the trail to the south.

The consensus among most prehistorians is that this trail, or rather several trails, were followed by expanding groups of rice farmers. Some of these groups may well have taken a coastal route, others would have followed the rivers that flow south and provide relatively easy access through the forested uplands they penetrate. The Red River and the Mekong are the two principal waterways, the Salween and the Chao Phraya are also relevant. After their passage through uplands of Vietnam and Laos, the flat plains of the Khorat Plateau, the Red River, Central Thailand and Cambodia must have seemed like a promised land.

What does the study of historic linguistics inform us on this proposed expansion? The majority of languages spoken today in Southeast Asia fall into a broad family known as Austro-Asiatic (AA). Khmer, Vietnamese and Mon are the dominant ones, but there are many others, and their distribution stretches from the coast of Vietnam into India. More recent arrivals into Southeast Asia include the Thai, who speak a non-AA language, and the Chams of Vietnam, who speak an Austronesian language. AA languages have many words in common, and these include rice, fish, child and dog. This in itself suggests a common origin. However, AA languages have also diverged over time. Although it is not possible to estimate with any accuracy the date when the ancestral languages split one from the other, most linguists agree that in the case of the widely distributed AA languages, several thousand years are in question.

The third source of information comes from the study of the ancestry of the modern population of Southeast Asia through sequencing their DNA. This relies on the fact that mutations in mitochondrial DNA and the non-recombining portion of the Y chromosome are inherited by all the same-sex descendants of the person in whom the mutation occurred, at least until another mutation occurs. Using data from living people, it is possible to construct a family tree showing where the different branches or descent lines formed. The study of DNA from prehistoric hunter-gatherers has barely begun, although mtDNA from skeletons in Moh Khiew Cave in Krabi Province of southern Thailand, dating to at least 11,000 and possibly as early as 25,000 years ago, suggests that they were ancestral to the modern Semang hunters of the same region (Oota et al. 2001). This finding, if substantiated, must be considered in conjunction with the findings of Hill et al. (2006), that the Semang mtDNA is compatible with a local ancestry stretching back about 50,000 years to the period when anatomically modern humans were first settling Southeast Asia. The key question in identifying migratory patterns involving Sundaland before 2000 BC, then, is to define the contribution made to the genetic make-up of modern populations. Although the pattern is not yet completely clear, there is little doubt that the indigenous hunter-gatherers interacted with intrusive rice farmers who moved into Southeast Asia from southern China, and contributed significantly to the gene pool (Mormina and Higham 2010).

However, the contribution to modern Southeast Asian inhabitants from hunter-gatherer populations is highly significant, and stresses that the expansion of Neolithic rice farmers was by no means a tsunami, but more a series of rivulets.

The inference to be drawn from the genetic data is that the rising sea by definition led to the migration of those living in both the inland and coastal tracts of Sundaland, and many may have moved north into what is now the mainland of Southeast Asia. A problem in documenting this possibility, is that relevant sites for defining the culture of the potential migrants are now under water. For millennia, the coastal communities would have been versed in seafaring, and the warm seas surrounding ancient Sundaland must be seen as highways to movement. Resettlement was axiomatic under the extreme environmental changes that took place over a period of at least 8,000 years until the sea level stabilized from about 1000 BC.

Summary

Four thousand years ago, Southeast Asia was occupied by many communities of hunter-gatherers whose ancestors had been adapting to the changing environments for over 50,000 years. Particularly rich and sedentary settlements were to be found along the shorelines formed when the sea was marginally higher than at present, while smaller and more mobile bands seasonally occupied rock shelters in the forested uplands. It is assumed that there were also settlements on the inland riverine plains, but these are yet to be identified and explored. It was into this already mature tradition of hunting and gathering, that the first rice farmers penetrated, to establish the cultural basis for a series of further profound changes in the structure of society.

3

Laying the Foundations

Introduction

A combination of archaeological and linguistic evidence strongly suggests that there was an expansion into Southeast Asia of rice farmers. A third source, genetics, requires caution, for there is a strong infusion of ancient, presumably hunter-gatherer, DNA in the genetic make-up of modern populations. On reflection, this is entirely to be expected. The intrusion of rice farmers necessitated interaction with hunter-gatherers whose ancestors had been attuned to the conditions of Southeast Asia for at least 2,500 generations. Consider other instances where two quite distinct cultural groups have interacted. It happened across the Americas, in Australia, indeed wherever European colonists met the indigenous inhabitants. Only very rarely, as in Tasmania and Argentina under an official policy, were the latter exterminated. We must therefore ask if there is any evidence for interaction and integration between the two different groups in Southeast Asia.

Relevant evidence again comes from several sources. The first is material culture. What did the different groups make, and how do their respective preferences differ. How did they bury their dead? Is there any evidence from the morphology of their bones, particularly the skull, that might point to two groups, or interbreeding. Might the sequencing of ancient DNA, or the isotopes in the teeth, help to distinguish between locals and newcomers?

A remarkable site: Khok Phanom Di

We have seen that Khok Phanom Di is one of the key sites in illuminating the rich life of hunter-gatherers in their estuarine habitat, but it also contains evidence for the interaction between the indigenous inhabitants and intrusive rice farmers. It was occupied during five centuries, between about 2000 and 1500 BC. Of the seven mortuary phases, the crucial phase 3 subdivided in two. The fact that the inhabitants from the initial settlement made fine pottery vessels and used polished stone adzes has encouraged some authorities to label them Neolithic. However, no domestic animals were found before the first dog bone appeared well into the cultural sequence Some fragments of rice were identified in exotic potsherds, but there is no guarantee that they were domesticated.

There was then a radical change with phase 3B. The sea level fell slightly and freshwater conditions developed. The isotopes in some women's teeth indicate that they were raised elsewhere. Shell knives were used probably to harvest rice, and heavy granite hoes were in use. The telling point is that domesticated rice remains have been found in human faeces and the digestive tract of a woman. At this stage in the cultural sequence, we also find that men and women were increasingly distinguished in death by their associated offerings, men with turtle carapaces, women with the craft tools for fashioning pottery vessels. This evidence suggests that some women came to Khok Phanom Di from Neolithic rice farming settlements in the interior. This integration brought the experience of rice production to the site, but with a rise in the sea level and reversion to saline conditions, the local cultivation of rice was short lived.

The interior plains: Ban Non Wat

Ban Non Wat is a key site in any consideration of the early Neolithic, because of the large area opened by excavation, and the tight chronology obtained through radiocarbon dating 76 samples, and then refining them through the Bayesian statistic known as OxCal 4.0 (Higham and Higham 2009). It is a large prehistoric settlement in the upper Mun Valley on the Khorat Plateau, ringed by two moats and banks. Such moated sites that concentrate in the Mun River valley were invariably occupied during the Iron Age, from the fifth century BC. However Ban Non Wat was also settled during both the Neolithic and Bronze Ages, and the cultural sequence has been divided into 12 successive phases.

The initial mortuary phase has all the hallmarks of the early Neolithic. The dead were placed in a supine position, associated with the characteristic I&I pottery vessels, and the bones of domestic pigs. Rice remains have been found in one grave and in the midden deposits. However, there is also a set of burials in which the dead were interred in a flexed, foetal position, and their mortuary offerings are quite distinct. In one case, a woman was found with shell beads fashioned more crudely than those associated with the Neolithic, and a woman wore large shell beads not found in any known Neolithic context. Just one pot was found with this group, and it is set apart from the Neolithic vessels by both its form and its lack of decoration. One woman was found on her back, again with the legs flexed, holding the skull of a pig, but others had no mortuary offerings at all. Dating the burials at this site has been undertaken on the basis of the freshwater shells that were placed in graves as mortuary offerings, and the results indicate initial Neolithic settlement in the seventeenth century BC. The radiocarbon dates for the separate flexed burials, however, show that they were contemporary not only with the Neolithic, but also down to the early Bronze Age. No DNA survives, and as yet there is no indication from the analysis of the shape of the crania that there were two different groups. However, the evidence available suggests that there was as at Khok Phanom Di, a form of integration between the indigenous inhabitants and the newcomers. If a flexed burial position in an otherwise Neolithic site can be taken further as a clue for the presence of hunter-gatherers, or at least their descendants, then several further sites present similar evidence. At Ban Chiang, which is located in the northeastern part of the same Khorat Plateau as Ban Non Wat, there was also an initial Neolithic presence, dated to the seventeenth century BC, but also a handful of flexed burials.

Man Bac and the Red River Delta

The lower reaches of the Red River in northern Vietnam lies in a highly strategic position for any movement south by rice farmers. The river itself links the region with Yunnan and ultimately the Yangtze, while the coast offers access from Guangdong and Guangxi provinces. Phung Nguyen is a key settlement that has given its name to the many Neolithic sites that cluster in this region, and Man Bac is one of these that has provided much new and vital information on the likely relationships between immigrants and the indigenous hunter gatherers. The site lies in a flat valley flanked by limestone towers, and was probably situated closer to the sea in prehistory. Excavations have yielded one of the largest samples of human burials from any similar site in Southeast Asia, and the skeletons are unusually complete and well preserved (Oxenham et al. 2010). The charcoal-based radiocarbon determinations suggest that the site was occupied from about 1900 BC.

The population biology has been assessed in several complementary studies. Visual inspection alone suggested that there are two groups of skull, one having a narrow and flat face, the other being lower and wider. To investigate these differences further, a series of measurements were taken and subjected to a statistical analysis in conjunction with samples of crania from other prehistoric sites, and with modern people (Matsumura 2010a). This is an analytical technique which does not find favour with all specialists in this field since there are factors other than genetic that can affect the shape of the head. However, the results from Man Bac are revealing. Nine of the Man Bac males analysed cluster in the results of the statistical analyses with the inhabitants of Neolithic Ban Chiang, the people of the later Iron Age and modern Vietnamese. On the other hand five individuals cluster with the earlier hunter-gatherers of this region. Most interestingly, the former group also clusters with the Neolithic inhabitants of the site of Weidun, which is an earlier agricultural community located in the Yangtze Valley.

The study of the cranium is not restricted to shape and measurements. There is also a series of non-metrical features that are genetically determined and therefore an informative approach to population histories. At Man Bac, Yukio Dodo (2010) has investigated six of these in order to identify similarities or differences with other sites and regions. The results place Man Bac closest to the Weidun people of the Yangtze basin, and furthest from a sample of Australian Aborigines. Dodo has concluded that the Man Bac crania reflect an intrusion from southern China ancestral to the modern Vietnamese.

Teeth are particularly durable, and their size and form at Man Bac have been considered relative to other samples, again with the added refinement of statistical analyses (Matsumura 2010b). On the basis of the crown diameter, the Man Bac people are closest to the modern Lao, and the prehistoric Chinese inhabitants of Weidun and Songze. They also differ markedly from the preceding hunter-gatherers from the sites of Con Co Ngua and Bac Son, as well as Andamanese and Australian Aborigines. As for the non-metric variables, they too link this site with a movement of immigrant rice farmers from southern

China, but not without some contribution from the indigenous hunter-gatherers.

Perhaps the most promising analytical method lies in the study of ancient DNA. DNA does not always survive from prehistoric contexts, particularly where conditions are typically hot and humid. Moreover, the amplification procedures are a minefield of difficulty due to the possibility of contamination with modern DNA. At Man Bac, however, Shinoda (2010) has been able to sequence mtDNA from some of the burials. It is evident that the cemetery contained individuals from several maternal lineages. Moreover, the haplogroups identified at the site suggest that there was indeed a southward movement of immigrants, and a local admixture with the indigenous inhabitants.

The importance of the Man Bac site lies in the consistent indication that the population incorporated immigrants from southern China who encountered and integrated with the long-established indigenous inhabitants. This harmonizes with the evidence from Ban Non Wat and Khok Phanom Di, as well as the indications from the DNA of modern inhabitants, of a significant contribution from hunter-gatherers. We can now turn to the archaeological evidence for the adaptation of the newcomers to the challenges of life in Southeast Asia.

Challenges for the first rice farmers

For any incoming group engaging with the lowlands of Southeast Asia, the environment would have presented some new and other old challenges. The climate as in much of southern China, is monsoonal. From early May, the prevailing wind direction comes from the southwest. This brings hot, humid conditions and heavy rainfall. The rainy season lasts until October or November, when the wind direction reverses, and cooler drier air from the northeast brings the dry season. The impact of the dry season varies from region to region.

Thus along the coast of Vietnam and the Red River Delta, the wind picks up moisture as it crosses the South China Sea, and there is still some rainfall. However, once over the Truong Son Cordillera, you enter the rain shadow of the Khorat Plateau and plains of Cambodia, and rainfall is negligible for months on end. A long dry season favours a Dipterocarp forest, in which deciduous trees predominate, giving way to a wetter gallery forest near the major waterways. With rising altitude and more rainfall, the forest becomes increasingly evergreen. Neolithic sites concentrate in the former. There, one finds a very rich and varied mammalian fauna. Herbivorous animals such as deer and cattle abound in nature. There are at least four species of deer varying from the large sambar to the small muntjak. The gaur, banteng and kouprey are indigenous cattle. Water buffalo are adapted to the lakes and marshes. There are also wild pigs, rhinoceros and elephant. The waterways harboured large crocodiles, and a huge range of fish and shellfish.

Ensuring a food supply was not, therefore, likely to have been a problem. The forest, however, would have been dominant beyond tracts that had been fired by the indigenous hunter-gatherers. Clearance was possible by burning, but some premium would also have been placed on securing a supply of high quality stone from which to fashion adzes. This would have permitted not only the creation of cleared areas and the construction of wooden houses, but also the opening of the forest to the cultivation of rice and millet, the two plants that they would have been accustomed to planting. This forested landscape was crossed by many rivers. On the Khorat Plateau, there are two major drainage basins fed by the Mun, Chi and Songkhram rivers. For Cambodia, the Great Lake was linked to the Mekong by the Tonle Sap River, while in Central Thailand, the Chao Phraya, Mae Klong and the Bang Pakong flow south into the Gulf of Siam. These rivers would have been the principal means of communication, linking settlements and encouraging exchange of desirable raw materials or finished artefacts.

A handful of Neolithic settlements have been excavated and published in sufficient detail for us to examine life during this formative stage of Southeast Asian prehistory. Ban Non Wat is located in the upper Mun Valley of Northeast Thailand, Man Bac is in northern Vietnam and An Son lies near the modern city of Saigon in the south of Vietnam. In Central Thailand, there are also Ta Kae, Non Pa Wai, Khok Charoen and Ban Kao.

The initial Neolithic settlement of Ban Non Wat took place in the seventeenth century BC. Archaeologically, it took the form of intact middens containing food refuse and artefacts, such as potsherds and stone adzes. In due course, human burials were cut down through these middens and often into the natural substrate. It is thought that Ban Non Wat was then slightly raised above the surrounding terrain and would have been less prone to flooding. The presence of rice itself documented in the middens by the presence of preserved husks, while the animal bones from these and the human burials include those of domesticated pigs and cattle. Dog bones are also found. The presence of dogs is important because they are ultimately descended from wolves. Since there are no indigenous wolves in Southeast Asia, the dog was absent from hunter-gatherer sites and only appeared when introduced, presumably from a Chinese source. There are a few bones from the water buffalo, but their size suggests that they were hunted rather than domesticated. Indeed, one of the features of subsistence was the numerical ascendancy of wild animals, particularly small, medium and large species of deer. The Javan rhinoceros is represented by two bones, and there are also some bones from the tiger and hare. Turtle remains abound. The presence of water buffalo and rhinoceros as well as the turtle bones point to the presence of low-lying wetlands near the site.

This receives support by the many fish bones and shellfish that dominate in the Neolithic middens. A sample from each cultural context was wet-sieved in order to retrieve the often tiny bones from fish. The bagrid catfish *Hemibagrus* and *Mystus* are the most abundant, with 142 individuals being represented. The snakehead, *Channa striata*, is also abundantly represented. There are 55 individuals of *Clarias* sp. while *Ompok* and *Wallago* account for 72. The fish identified in the Neolithic middens of Ban Non Wat confirm the presence of an aquatic environment that could contribute significantly to sustaining a relatively large sedentary community.

The dominant shellfish are *Filopaludina* and *Pila*. Both gastropods are known to inhabit freshwater ponds and lakes, and in the case of the former, streams. They are widely consumed today in Northeast Thailand, particularly during the wet season, for *Pila ampullacea* aestivate if water dries out and are not easy to find in quantities since they can bury themselves to a depth of up to a metre. Bivalve shellfish were also a significant part of the Neolithic diet. *Ensidens ingalsianus* was the most abundant, followed by *Scabies* sp. These come from river and lake beds, and are still collected and put on sale in the regional market places of Northeast Thailand.

Human burials are a second source of information on the initial Neolithic settlement of Ban Non Wat. Radiocarbon determinations on the shellfish placed with the dead indicate that they were interred in the fourteenth century BC. Two adults, a man and a woman, had been placed in a large, lidded ceramic vessel, seated upright in a crouched position. The remaining adults had been laid on the back. Infants were found within lidded pots. Ceramic vessels were the principal mortuary offering. One person wore shell bead necklace, and another was found with a single shell bangle. Two individuals were accompanied by cowrie shells. A young man wore these as ear ornaments. No such associations suggesting use as jewellery were identified with the five cowrie shells associated with the woman interred in a pottery vessel. Animal offerings were found in the form of pig and fish bones, the latter contained in ceramic vessels. Four stone adzes were also placed with burials. In a tradition that endured for 2,000 years at this site, right into the Iron Age,

4 adults were also buried with large bivalve shells that to judge from their careful placement, were probably of symbolic importance.

The techniques for decorating the pottery vessels, and the preferred designs, are an important means of identifying relationships with the occupants of other Neolithic sites. The potters of Ban Non Wat were extremely skilful, and the presence of clay anvils in Neolithic contexts, used to shape the wet clay, indicate local manufacture. To make a vessel large enough to contain a grown man or woman, and then apply to it incised and painted designs embellished further with burnished bands suggest a long ancestral tradition. Pots placed with the dead were made in a variety of forms, and again were embellished with panels of complex incised designs infilled with impressions or red paint (Figure 3.1). The motifs include one that resembles a human figure, two others have been described as a whale and a sickle. Even the interior bases of pedestalled pots have been painted in complex, swirling designs (Higham and Wiriyaromp 2011).

Other artefacts found in occupation layers expand further on the activities and the relationships of this Neolithic community. One of the most significant is the spindle whorl. No such artefacts, which are used to produce thread prior to weaving, are known in hunter-gatherer contexts. They were, however, employed among the Neolithic communities of the Yangtze Valley. One of those found at Ban Non Wat is biconical, and its form can be traced back to such sites as Tanshishan in Southeast China. There were also many stone adze heads, vital for any approach to cutting back the forest to create living space and rice fields. Over 200 adzes were recovered, and two forms predominated, one with a shoulder and one oval and non-shouldered. Most were made from a basalt that has been sourced both to the Phetchabun range, 130 km west of the site, or from high terraces 50 km to the south. The presence of manuports of basalt, that is unmodified lumps of raw material matched in the latter area, has suggested that the inhabitants of Ban Non Wat could well have had direct access to this source. The adzes were valued: few have been

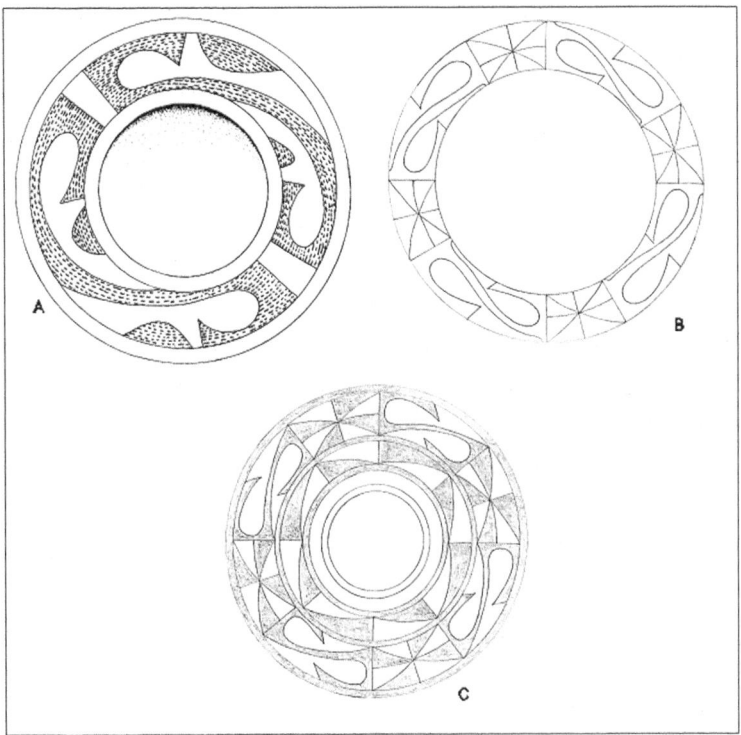

Figure 3.1 Incised and impressed designs link early Neolithic sites in Southeast Asia. These incorporate a human-like figure. A: Khok Phanom Di, B: Khok Charoen and C: Sab Champa.

found with burials, and many were sharpened so regularly that they ultimately were worn down to a small size while still used (Boer-Mah 2011). This harmonizes with the number of well-used whetstones that co-vary with the adze heads.

Man Bac

Man Bac in northern Vietnam was occupied between about 1800–1400 BC, the same time as the early Neolithic at Ban Non Wat, and was in many respects similar. In terms of basic subsistence, there was at Man Bac the same mixture between the introduction of domestic pigs and the continuation of hunting and gathering. Interestingly, it might be that some of the pigs were locally domesticated, rather than introduced, by settlers already conversant with the idea of animal domestication. They were numerically dominant with just over half of all mammals identified. Dogs were also present and presumably introduced. Deer represent 13.5 per cent of the sample, and there are also a small number of bovid and rhinoceros bones. Fish were also abundant, but unlike Ban Non Wat, the majority came from a marine habitat. The most common species was the black sea bream with just over half the sample. As at Khok Phanom Di sharks and rays were also brought in from the open sea. No rice has been reported from this site, but the excavators, given the high incidence of dental caries, have suggested that the diet might have included root crops such as the taro.

The burials also provide parallels and differences from Ban Non Wat. There are no jar burials, neonates to the elderly were interred in a supine position, although one adult was found with arms and legs flexed. Bivalve shells, for example, were clearly of ritual importance. They were found on several occasions, held in each hand of the deceased. The dominant mortuary offering was the pottery vessel. Many from all age groups were accompanied by a single pot, the most was eight, found with an adult man. In terms of ornaments, several people were associated with cowrie shells or nephrite beads often found as necklaces, while T-cross sectioned nephrite bangles were rare. One was found with a young man described as the richest interment found. He also had cowrie shells, a bivalve shell and three pottery vessels (Huffer and Trinh Hoang Hiep 2010). The predominant impression gained from this cemetery is a uniformity of treatment in death from infants to the aged. The few individuals who stand out in terms of mortuary offerings cannot by any yardstick be described as particularly wealthy.

The mortuary vessels are dominated in form by globular bowls with a constricted neck, and its surface decoration by grooves running round or down the vessel and referred to as ribbing. There are also a very small number of more complex forms decorated with incised and impressed patterns. These, judging from their fabric, might well have been imported from a source with a ceramic tradition more centrally within the Phung Nguyen tradition of I&I decoration. The closest parallels to the majority of bowls are found along the coast of southern China and in particular, the Hong Kong region towards the end of the third millennium BC. It would seem that the immigrant component of the Man Bac population might have reached the Red River Delta by a coastal route in the first two or three centuries of the second millennium BC.

An Son

An Son is one of several Neolithic settlements located in the valley of the Vam Co Dong River, 60 km northwest of Saigon. It is particularly relevant to any understanding of the timing and the nature of Neolithic settlement in Southeast Asia because it was occupied for about a millennium, and extensive excavations have not yielded any evidence for copper-base metallurgy. The radiocarbon determinations come not only from charcoal, which has limited value due to the distorting influence of inbuilt age, but also from the human remains themselves. These suggest initial occupation at or just after 2000 BC, and abandonment in the eleventh century BC. It was thus occupied at the same time as Khok Phanom Di and Neolithic Ban Non Wat (Bellwood et al. n.d.).

The biological remains have illuminated the subsistence base for this Neolithic community (Piper et al. 2012). During the second to the fourth of the four occupation phases, pottery vessels were tempered with rice chaff, and an analysis of the DNA of this rice shows it to be *Oryza japonica*, the species that was brought under domestication in China. The domestic animals are dominated numerically by the dog, which again is thought to have originated in China. Some of these canid bones bear cut marks reflecting butchering, and were then, as now in Vietnam, raised for their meat. Pigs are next in terms of abundance. Again, local wild pigs might have been domesticated initially, but in due course the dominance of animals killed when aged 12–18 months suggests that by 1800–1600 BC, they were a managed population. Cattle are absent, but some hunting was undertaken for deer. The importance of wet sieving a sample of cultural material is demonstrated by the recovery of a large sample of fish bones that would otherwise have been missed due to their small size. Although the sea would then have been within reach of An Son, freshwater fish dominate, led by the swamp eel, the climbing perch and the snakehead. There are also many fragments of water turtle bones.

The material culture falls into place as typical of the Southeast Asian Neolithic. Stone adze heads, some shouldered and others not, were probably imported to the site, since there is no evidence for fashioning them locally. However, they were regularly sharpened and repaired. There are also bone fishhooks as at Khok Phanom Di, pellet bow pellets and burnishing stones for polishing the surface of pottery vessels prior to firing. The pottery vessels themselves include round-based bowls and other bowls raised on pedestals. There are also dishes with an unusual wavy rim. Decoration included I&I designs typical of the initial Neolithic.

Burials were distributed through much of the excavated area, as at Ban Non Wat without the tight nucleation into groups seen at Khok Phanom Di. The dead were placed in a supine position, usually accompanied by a handful of pots. Stone adzes were on occasion placed in the grave, while personal ornaments, such as shell beads, were rare. An examination of the shape of the crania matches the occupants of this site with Iron Age and modern Vietnamese, but the dentition has more affinities with the preceding Hoabinhian hunter-gatherers, as at Man Bac suggesting a mixed population.

Central Thailand

Central Thailand also contains a number of Neolithic settlements. Non Pa Wai is best known for its thick deposit of copper-smelting debris, but this overlies a Neolithic occupation and cemetery that stretches beyond the later complex. The 35 burials uncovered there reflect the widespread custom of interment on the back, with a range of mortuary offerings that at this site, include fine I&I pots, marble pendants, stone adze heads, H-shaped and disc shell beads and bivalve shells. The H beads are identical with those from the penultimate mortuary phase at Khok Phanom Di, and thus probably date to the seventeenth or sixteenth century BC. Again, the prominent human figure motif incised on the surface of the pottery vessels at Non Pa Wai is matched on a vessel from this Khok Phanom Di during the final mortuary phase. Flotation at this site to recover plant remains has yielded a large and impressive sample of seeds. Most unexpectedly, the dominant domestic plant represented is *Setaria italica*, the foxtail millet, while rice in the early Neolithic contexts is absent (Weber et al. 2010). This plant was native to and originally domesticated in northern China, and its presence in Central Thailand lends strong support to the model for Chinese stimulus in the Southeast Asian Neolithic. One of the millet seeds has been radiocarbon dated to the late third millennium BC, which is rather earlier than anticipated. More determinations are needed to pinpoint the timing of initial settlement.

Tha Kae lies to the southwest of Non Pa Wai, and the excavators have suggested that the Neolithic occupation there took place between about 1800 and 1100 BC. Here again, there are inhumation burials with I&I pottery vessels, and others cord-marked or painted with red geometric patterns. Some of the forms of pot at these two sites also match those from Ban Non Wat. Both sites also have bivalve shells, shell disc beads and infants interred in lidded vessels, although ceramic stoves at Tha Kae are not known in the upper Mun Valley.

Ban Kao was the first Neolithic site in Thailand to be excavated (Sørensen and Hatting 1967). It lies near two tributaries of the Khwae Noi River. Forty-two human burials have been excavated, and according to the associated charcoal-based radiocarbon determinations, the site was occupied in the first half of the second millennium BC. The mortuary offerings included pottery vessels in a variety of forms, the most distinctive being a bowl raised on three conical legs. There are also stone adze heads, disc-shaped beads of shell and bivalve shells. Many men and women were also accompanied by the articulating limb bones of domestic pigs. The tripod pots have been found further south into Malaysia, and Sørensen has suggested that the ancestral forms were made in China with the Salween as a likely conduit for the expansion south of farming communities.

Khok Charoen was also excavated during the early phase of enquiry into the Neolithic. Located in an intermediate low-lying river valley between Central and Northeast Thailand, the 44 human burials reflect the identical mortuary practices already seen. Pottery vessels were decorated with similar motifs employing the same I&I techniques. Shell jewellery of marine origin could have been exported from Khok Phanom Di, so similar are the shapes. There are stone adze heads and stone beads. One burial at this site is markedly richer than most Neolithic burials, for it contained no fewer than 19 pottery vessels, 10 shell and 9 stone bracelets and many shell disc beads.

However, the evidence of both archaeology and genetics stress that this was not a wave of new settlement that ran roughshod over the indigenous hunter-gatherers. The DNA of the latter still contribute significantly to the present genetic make-up of Southeast

Asia, and the evidence of human bones and teeth points to a mixed population in the new Neolithic villages. At Khok Phanom Di and Ban Non Wat, the mortuary traditions reflect local as well as exotic customs. Hunting, fishing and gathering continued to be significant contributors to the subsistence base. Linguistically, the widespread distribution of Austroasiatic languages sharing cognate words for rice and aspects of its cultivation, together with the time necessary for the various languages to have diverged, supports the model of southern expansion.

These Neolithic communities proliferated over a period of at least seven centuries as the population grew. They form the essential bedrock upon which all further cultural changes were founded.

4

The Coming of the Age of Bronze

A debate on timing

Debates on the timing, origin and significance of the adoption of bronze metallurgy in Southeast Asia have swirled through the literature for almost half a century. It all began in 1965, when Ernestine Green, a graduate student of Wilhelm G. Solheim II, opened a test square at a small mounded site called Non Nok Tha in Northeast Thailand. She encountered human burials, and a sandstone bivalve mould for casting a socketed bronze axe. A large excavation the following year revealed a burial with a socketed bronze axe as a mortuary offering, and another grave containing an adult wearing bronze bangles. In his report on this season, Solheim (1968) stressed the difficulty of dating a site where there was much disturbance through the digging of graves, and the scarcity of charcoal. However, he cited two radiocarbon determinations for a lower level at the site as being evidence for bronze casting by about 2500 BC. He placed this in the then context of Southeast Asian prehistory by noting that hitherto, the earliest evidence for bronze metallurgy was in the late first millennium BC in the Dong Son culture of northern Vietnam. Further excavations in 1968 enlarged the number of burials, and associated bronzes. A new set of radiocarbon determinations based on fragments of charcoal suggested to Solheim (1972) that copper smelting and alloying began by the mid-fourth millennium BC.

In 1974–5, the timing and the nature of the initial Bronze Age was reopened by two seasons of excavations at the site of Ban Chiang, a modestly sized mound located 118 km northeast of Non Nok Tha. Again, burials were found containing bronze offerings: one man was found with a socketed spear, a child wore bronze anklets. The later graves also contained iron items. In situ charcoal was again scarce, and most radiocarbon determinations came from fragments accumulated from grave fill. In their preliminary report, the excavators employed the C14 results to suggest that bronzes were in use by about 3600 BC, with iron appearing between 1600–1200 BC (Gorman and Charoenwongsa 1976). This encouraged Bayard, who had directed the 1968 excavation at Non Nok Tha, to conclude that: 'I believe that the recent Ban Chiang evidence makes it highly likely that bronze metallurgy was well developed before 3000 BC' (Bayard 1980).

The implications of these claims are profound. If true, then Northeast Thailand would have to be seen as an independent centre of the discovery of copper base metallurgy. It would run counter to the widespread and well-documented origins in eastern Turkey and the Levant, and the subsequent spread of this technology out from the seminal area. However, balanced criticism was not long in coming. Loofs-Wissowa adroitly identified the questionable contexts from which the dated charcoal was derived, and concluded that 'As can be seen, the state of research into early metals in Southeast Asia is one of utter turmoil' (Loofs-Wissowa 1983: 10). I excavated the site of Ban Na Di in 1982. This prehistoric mound is located only 20 km south of Ban Chiang and their Bronze Age sequences partially overlap. Our charcoal samples were large, and derived from unquestioned contexts, such as the clay furnaces used to liquefy copper. The results were significantly later than those claimed for Ban Chiang (Higham 1983).

Establishing an acceptable chronological framework has taken many twists and turns over the last 40 years. Having assumed responsibility for the analysis and publication of the Ban Chiang excavations, Joyce White first revisited the charcoal-based chronology, concluding that bronze working was established there between 1700–2100 BC (White 1982). She went on to stress that 'The discovery of a distinctive metallurgical tradition in Southeast Asia at least comparable to that of northern China, if not earlier, has added new pieces to the puzzle of metallurgical origins' (White 1982: 48). Subsequently, resolution of this problem has taken advantage of new radiocarbon dating methods. It is in all such research, crucial that the object being dated is in unarguable association with the event for which a determination is sought. Charcoal, even if from a totally secure context, is suspect unless it comes from a short-lived species, because of the problem of inbuilt age. Imagine a Bronze Age farmer chopping down an old tree and using some of the wood for cooking. If the wood in question comes from inner growth rings, it will have what is known as inbuilt age, and give therefore a spuriously early date. The unreliability of mixed samples of charcoal from hearths is well documented (Ashmore 1999).

Accelerator mass spectroscopy dating opened new possibilities for re-dating sites, because it requires tiny samples, compared with the bulky charcoal needed previously. It seemed as if this technique would prove a panacea, for the dead at Ban Chiang and Non Nok Tha were interred with pottery vessels tempered with rice chaff. Isolating carbonized rice from within the pot matrix should surely provide a reliable result. This was taken up with relief and enthusiasm in Southeast Asia. I employed the technique to date the Bronze Age cemetery of Nong Nor (Higham and Thosarat 1998). Glover did likewise at Ban Don Ta Phet. I obtained samples of non-mortuary sherds from Non Nok Tha for dating at Oxford University. The results were markedly later than the fourth millennium, most falling between 1400–900 BC (Higham 1996: 191). Joyce White has also obtained AMS determinations from rice chaff extracted from

Neolithic and Bronze Age mortuary vessels at Ban Chiang (White 1997, 2008).

As experimental procedures have been applied to this method of dating, so a number of key problems have been identified. Foremost is the simple fact that the clay used in making a pot can itself contain carbon. There is also the possibility that the pot might have absorbed carbon from the smoke generated during the firing procedure. There is now a shelf of papers warning against the application of this procedure (Hedges et al. 1992, Bonsall et al. 2002, Berstan et al. 2008). This difficulty is elegantly illustrated by White's own results (Glusker and White 1997). Two principal pretreatments were applied to the potsherds selected for dating. In one (treatment A), fragments of organic matter were teased out of the potsherd and treated with acetone, 0.2 N HCl and 0.5 N NaOH successively to extract lipids, carbonates and humic acids. In the second pretreatment (treatment B) the above procedure was applied to crushed potsherds, and followed by either a mixture of 4 M HF in 6 M HCl or concentrated hydrofluoric acid followed by multiple washings. This procedure '*aims to concentrate the carbon content of the residue and also makes soluble a considerable quantity of clay-bound humic material*'. The offset between the two forms of pretreatment is often huge. Thus, a pot from burial 12 under treatment A is 1970±60 BP while that for treatment B is 2980±50 BP. Again, a vessel from burial 19/24 has provided a treatment A determination of 2190±70 BP and 2545±65 for treatment B. In the event, White has chosen the results under treatment B, that which invariably furnishes the earliest date, as the preferable method. These, she has concluded, indicate that the Bronze Age at Ban Chiang began between 1800–2000 BC (White and Hamilton 2009).

This proposed date has furthered the long-running debate on Bronze Age chronology and its implications. To the specialist and the neutral observer alike, it must seem extraordinary that this one site should harbour bronze founder specialists some centuries before the initial Neolithic settlement of Southeast Asia as set out in the previous chapter. Nevertheless, White and Hamilton have developed a model that identifies the stimulus to the bronze casting tradition at Ban Chiang in the Seima-Turbino cultural phenomenon. The sites of this group stretch from the Altai Mountains to Finland. To reach Ban Chiang as well would have entailed a long march of over 2,500 km, along a route ran across the grain of western China. If true, then there would have been a 1,000-year span at Ban Chiang during which there was little if any cultural change resulting from the adoption there of metallurgy.

Resolving the dating debate

A vital lead finally to resolve this debate comes from the site of Ban Non Wat. Like Ban Chiang and Non Nok Tha, settlement began with the Neolithic, followed by a transition into the Bronze Age. Unlike those two sites, it also lies on a major exchange route linking Central Thailand with its copper sources with the broad expanse of the Khorat Plateau. My son, the Deputy Director of the AMS radiocarbon dating laboratory at Oxford, began dating this site by employing charcoal from hearths, but we then turned to the freshwater bivalve shells that were placed with the dead. The 76 determinations were then analysed using Bayesian statistics. The result pinpointed the transition from the late Neolithic into the Bronze Age in the late eleventh century BC. The dilemma we then confronted was the thousand-year gap between this date and that for early bronze at Ban Chiang. The only way of resolving it, we concluded, was to employ the latest ultrafiltration pretreatment for bone and date the human skeletons from Ban Chiang. We would have preferred this approach at Ban Non Wat, but there was no collagen in the bones. Fortunately, the Ban Chiang bones yielded up sufficient collagen to date. We found that the earliest burial

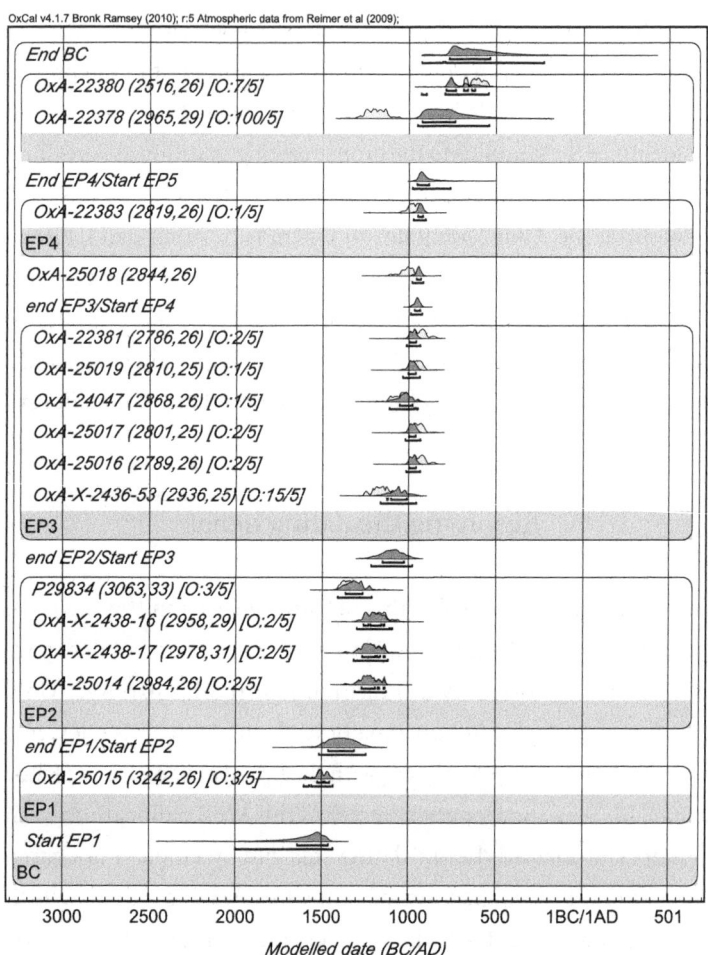

Figure 4.1 The radiocarbon determinations on human and animal bone from Ban Chiang. EP1 is the earliest Neolithic, EP2 is later Neolithic, EP3 is initial Bronze Age, EP4–5 are later Bronze Age. The results show that the transition into the Bronze Age at this site took place in the eleventh century BC.

with a finished bronze artefact has a date of 1128–936 BC. Another early individual was accompanied by a small piece of bronze, and the date is 1026–900 BC (Figure 4.1). The dates as a whole form an almost perfect match with those of Ban Non Wat (Higham et al. 2011).

Origins

While the claims for a third millennium context for bronze casting at Ban Chiang were current, there was a severe disarticulation in the pattern of early metallurgy in Eurasia as a whole. This arises as a result of the growing body of evidence for a progressive spread of copper base skills from west to east that was to reach north and central lowlands of China by the early second millennium BC. The implication of the putative early Bronze Age dates would be that there was a second centre of innovation, or at least a remarkable transmission of the knowledge of bronze casting from the Altai to Ban Chiang that left no footprint in China.

The end of the debate on the chronology makes it possible to position the Southeast Asian Bronze Age in its proper perspective. As Roberts et al. (2009) have shown, an interest in the properties of native metals and their ores as ornaments began as early as the eleventh to the ninth millennia in the area between Israel, northern Iraq and eastern Turkey. By 8000 BC, native copper and copper ore were being modified through the application of heat at the site of Cayönü Tepesi. The pattern in the core area over the next three millennia was one of increasing application of heat to smelting and casting, and the outward spread of founding expertise. By the late fifth and early fourth millennia, copper ore containing a fraction of arsenic or lead was being exploited in Southwest and Central Asia, providing thereby a natural alloy. This was followed in the former area by the first casting of tin bronzes. Tin has the effect, if present in a proportion of about 1:10 with copper, to harden the resulting alloy. The next major expansion towards the east involved communities in Northwest China which, through exchange contact with the steppe, were casting small items of bronze in the early centuries of the third millennium. Having reached the western portal to the Yellow

River Neolithic settlements, we then find the adoption of bronze technology in the Xia and Shang dynasties. Here, as in virtually all other instances in this expansionary process, the technology saw innovations to meet consumer demands. In the case of the Shang, piece-mould casting was employed to create sumptuary bronzes that would have advertised royal prestige. But there was also a parallel tradition of casting useful tools and weapons using bivalve moulds. By the thirteenth century BC, a highly distinctive and particularly impressive bronze casting tradition developed further south in the Yangtze Valley, where at Sanxingdui, massive human masks and other ritual items were cast, including a tree.

At this juncture, as we have seen, Southeast Asia was populated with small Neolithic communities. Some of these were either directly or through intermediaries, exchanging goods with the burgeoning states of China. The latter highly valued cowrie shells as symbols of wealth, and turtle shell to undertake their divinations. Both could be supplied from the far south. The Neolithic communities best placed to respond to these demands geographically lie in Lingnan, the southernmost provinces of China, and northern Vietnam. And predictably, it was in these very regions that we find items that originated in the early states, such as jade *yazhang* blades and bronzes. These southward links have been set out in detail (Ciarla 2007, Pigott and Ciarla 2007, Higham et al. 2011). Roberts et al. (2007) have stressed two important points. The first is that acquiring metallurgical expertise involves so many complex procedures, that it must have involved the movement of experienced and skilled founders. Secondly, as it spread progressively from the Near East ultimately to reach Southeast Asia, so founders responded to local demands in what they cast. It is, therefore, at this juncture that we can turn to the impact that this vital technological innovation had on the late Neolithic communities of Southeast Asia who, in the late eleventh century, were becoming familiar with the properties of copper and tin.

Social change in the Bronze Age

Until the excavation of Ban Non Wat in Northeast Thailand, nearly all the excavations of Bronze Age sites opened only a modest area. As a result, we still have no clear idea of how big an area a settlement covered, how many people it might have harboured and where people actually lived. Most information on the social life of the Bronze Age people comes from cemeteries rather than living areas, and again, unless one exposes a reasonably large area, the amount of information available is bound to be limited. Thus, the 1975 excavation at Ban Chiang was a mere 3.5 m wide, and covered an area of only 99m². My excavations at Ban Na Di in 1982 were even smaller. When reviewing the available information before the seven seasons of work at Ban Non Wat, there was very little evidence for changes in society from any site. The Bronze Age burials at Ban Chiang contained few mortuary offerings. At Ban Na Di, one group was consistently wealthier, in terms of exotic jewellery and other grave goods, than a second, contemporary group, but not markedly so. At Non Nok Tha, the mortuary offerings were dominated by pottery vessels, and there were very few bronzes or exotic ornaments.

Nevertheless, several working models have been proposed. All have been anchored on the fact that no exposure of a cemetery has provided evidence for an elite social group distinguished by unusual mortuary wealth and a restricted location. As White and Pigott (1996) have noted, 'No Northeast Thai site has revealed a distinct, isolated area exclusively for well-endowed graves'. While some individuals were richer than others, there is more a continuum of wealth than a demarcation. In 1989, arguing from the results of very limited information, I suggested that Bronze Age settlements were autonomous, and that 'the attainment of status was flexible rather than fixed, and that the relative position of each autonomous settlement was given to fluctuation, and therefore instability' (Higham 1989).

This prediction has subsequently been elaborated through the notion of heterarchy (White 1995, O'Reilly 2003). White (1995: 101) began her study by relating the late development of states in Southeast Asia to the 'long term presence of two technological and economic factors sometimes considered important to state formation elsewhere: i) cultivation since the fourth millennium BC of a cereal (rice), . . . and production of copper-base metals dating at least from the first half of the second millennium BC'. As we have seen, these dates may now be set aside.

From the numerous attributes of a heterarchical social organization, White singled out the following as characteristic of Bronze Age Southeast Asia: production of objects was undertaken at the household level. Whether it be ceramics, cloth, shell, stone or metal, there was no elite organization of specialists. There was no preferential access to or ownership of valuables employed to indicate status. The wide and generalized distribution of resources meant that there was no elite control over exchange. Nor is there any evidence for conflict or warfare that might indicate competition for resources. Communities were self-contained with their own preferences, as seen in White's comparison of the contemporary expressions of Bronze Age mortuary behaviour at two nearby sites in Northeast Thailand, Ban Chiang and Ban Na Di. Although only 20 km apart, their pottery vessels are quite different one from the other. O'Reilly (2003), in his interpretation of the Bronze Age cemetery of Ban Lum Khao, found in the absence of significant differences in mortuary wealth indicating high status individuals, support for White's model of heterarchy.

The new information from Ban Non Wat has opened a new dimension to the debate (Higham 2011). Six phases of Bronze Age occupation of the site occupy about 600 years, say 30 human generations, that follow on directly from the late Neolithic, and in due course merge into the early Iron Age. Although only seven burials represent Bronze Age (BA) 1 at this site, they provide vital clues on the social changes that then took place. The late Neolithic pottery vessels were dominated by round based, cord-marked bowls lacking the I&I decoration of their predecessors. Very similar bowls were found with the BA1 individuals but they were much more skilfully finished. Moreover, there were many more of them, an average of 14 in each grave against under 2 in the late Neolithic. Graves were dug much more deeply than hitherto and were more elaborate. One woman was interred in a wooden coffin with a boat-like prow. She wore over 2,000 shell disc beads, probably of marine origin, in the form of a belt and necklaces. Most significantly, she was also accompanied by a socketed copper-base axe. Mortuary wealth was not confined to adults. An infant was interred in a wooden coffin under a layer of gastropod shellfish. Seventeen pottery vessels were grouped beyond the head and feet, and the infant wore six marine trochus shell bangles. A 10-year-old had been interred with a copper-base axe. Not only did these people own copper-base axes, they also had access to a much greater quantity of exotic shell jewellery and interred their dead with a more intensive set of rituals that included placing pig bones and bivalve shells in the graves.

BA1 according to the radiocarbon determinations, probably did not last for more than a couple of generations. With BA2, the cemetery contained rows of burials so wealthy that they can reasonably be described as princely. Moreover, they contain the remains of men, women and infants so probably represent one or more descent lines that used this cemetery over a period of about 150 years. The ten male burials range from very young to old individuals. Graves were deeply excavated, and far larger than was necessary to contain the coffin. The extra space was employed to accommodate ceramic vessels and other offerings. There is a greater variety of forms and many were elaborately decorated with complex and sophisticated red-painted designs. The number of vessels is markedly larger than at any other Bronze Age site in Southeast Asia, with an average of 30 per burial. Burials 20/90, contained in the same grave, were accompanied by 73. The longest grave, that of an old male, contained 40.

The weight of ornaments was also a quantum leap over BA1. All but one man wore exotic marine trochus shell bangles. Burial 571 wore 53, and the average is 25. Six men also wore tridacna shell bangles. They shared between them, 17 marble bangles. Shell disc beads are laborious to manufacture, and may reflect personal wealth. Burial 197, a mid to old man, wore nearly 10,000 and the average is nearly 3500 (Figure 4.2). Some men also wore shell earrings. Six of the ten men were accompanied by at least one copper-base artefact. Socketed axes in three distinct forms predominated. One man was also buried with a tanged copper-base chisel. Three chisels, an awl and two axes had been placed with burial 197. They look like a set of wood-working tools. Copper-base ornaments were rare. There were no bangles, but one young man wore 25 bells. In terms of ritual offerings, most men were buried with bivalve shells and caches of red ochre. Rituals also involved exhuming at least two men some time after the interment, and then replacing the bones neatly in the grave. Were these people revered ancestors whose physical remains projected mana?

The seven female graves were far larger than was necessary to contain a coffin, to make space for ceramic vessels. Burials 105 and 106 lay alongside each other in the same large grave and were accompanied by 89 pottery vessels of great diversity of form and size. The average number of vessels with women is 31. Exotic marine shell bangles were worn by all women, the youngest having 41. Burial 105 is an old adult who was interred with 13 tridacna shell bangles. Three women also possessed marble bangles, and two wore shell earrings. Women wore more shell disc beads than men, 19,410 being found with the old women in burial 105, worn as multiple strands of necklaces and belts. Copper-base items were confined to two axes. Probable ritual offerings include bivalve shells and blood-red ochre. Again, two of these women in burials 93 and 106 had been partially exhumed some

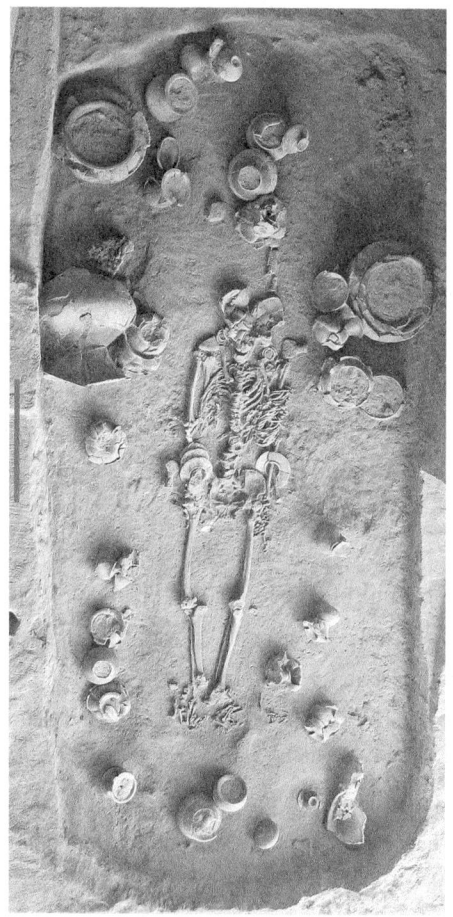

Figure 4.2 Burial 197 at Ban Non Wat contained a Bronze Age male grandee, interred with immense wealth in terms of ceramic vessels, shell jewellery and copper artefacts.

time after the primary interment, the bones then being replaced in the grave.

The 14 infant burials display intense mortuary rituals. Two were foetal, two were newly born, the remainder died when between eight months and five years of age. Burial 550 was contained in a lidded jar. The infant within was aged 27–32 weeks from conception. The jar contained five ceramic vessels and a bivalve shell. The newly born infant in burial 406, a second lidded jar burial, was accompanied by seven miniature pots. The mortuary jar and lid are very large and impressive in form. A second neonate was interred in a similar lidded vessel. The lid interior was painted in a complex design that might represent birth. Two small pots, a bivalve shell and red ochre had been placed within. The last jar burial, which was painted all over with curvilinear designs, contained the remains of an infant who died when aged about 9–12 months.

The burial of the other infants closely followed the rituals that attended adult men and women. Graves were invariably far larger than necessary for the body alone, and the areas beyond the feet and the head contained groups of ceramic vessels and other mortuary offerings. Two infants were buried with socketed copper-base axes, and five bells accompanied burial 468. Pig's limb bones were found with six of the infants, and in terms of ritual or symbolic objects, bivalve shells and red ochre were common. Burial 293 is a good example of the energy expended on these infants. The grave itself is 4 m in length for the tiny body. The infant wore large tridacna shell bangles, and shell disc bead earrings. The skeleton was covered in shell beads. Two bivalve shells were carefully positioned over the left hand and the severed foot bones of two pigs lay among the pots beyond the feet.

The opulent rituals that attended burials continued into the succeeding phase, BA3B, although the orientation of the graves changed. The graves were laid out in rows, and involved 7 women, 5 men, an adult and an infant interred over a period in the region of 50 years. The wealth expressed in terms of exotic shell jewellery is remarkable. One man wore 65 trochus shell bangles, and a woman 62. Another man's arms were covered in bangles – 54 of trochus and 18 cut from tridacna shell (Figure 4.3). An adult was found to have worn nearly 24,000 shell disc beads, and other ornaments included long shell beads, shell and marble earrings. Copper base items comprised a socketed axe and anklets incorporating rings. The only infant wore anklets embellished with 30 copper base bells. Numerous ceramic

Figure 4.3 Burial 260 at Ban Non Wat. This man was weighed down the trochus shell bangles that had to be imported over many hundreds of kilometres from a clear coral sea.

vessels in a variety of forms filled the graves together with red ochre, bivalve shells and the articulating limb bones of pigs.

As one proceeds to the south in the excavated area, graves in this same group and on the same orientation during BA3B revealed a sharp decline in the number of mortuary offerings placed with the dead. This group comprised six men, five women, two adults and seven infants. The number of offerings with this group when compared with the corresponding figures for BA3A tell a clear story of decline. Although the number of burials in each is about the same, the number of exotic shell bangles fell from 361 to 79, bronzes from 36 to 1, marble bangles from 19 to 3 and shell beads from 78,271 to 4,035. Yet the basic mortuary ritual of interment in a supine position with the placement of pottery vessels, bivalve shells, pig bone and jewellery continued unchanged.

The fourth phase of the Bronze Age, dated to the eighth century BC, involved burials across the entire excavated area. Graves were located in rows, but also in long columns with the dead placed head to toe in five possible groups. Forty-three men were identified, 45 women and 54 infants or children. The basic rituals of death continued, but again, relative poverty ruled for most, although a handful of individuals stand out for their relative wealth. Burial 280 for example, contained a 10-year-old child and was quite elaborate. Larger than necessary to contain the child's coffin, it was associated with ten ceramic vessels including a pot that bears comparison with the finest from BA2. There was also a marble bangle, very rarely found in this group, and three trochus shell bangles. Bronzes were rare to the point of being virtually absent, which is surprising given the mortuary offerings found with a young to mid-aged man in burial 549, interred with 29 clay moulds, for casting socketed axes and bangles. It is highly likely that he was a specialist bronze founder (Higham 2008). The moulds for casting the bangles even display an element of mass production. They were employed in a row, rather like books on a shelf, and the molten metal would have been decanted into five or more moulds in one operation. Although surely a specialist, his other mortuary offerings only comprised a couple of pottery vessels.

The last phase of the Bronze Age fell within the span 700–420 BC. Ten men were identified, 14 women, 5 adults and 6 infants or children.

While ceramic vessel forms evolved, the basic mortuary tradition continued, with the grave orientated on an approximate north to south axis, although in some cases, the body faced to the south rather than to the north. One hundred and six pots were found with the adults, an average of just over four each. We now find that spindle whorls and grey clay were placed with the dead. Since whorls were used to create yarn, and grey clay can be used as a dye or mordant, there is a strong likelihood that this community developed a special interest in the production of cloth.

Shell beads and bangles became extremely rare, and marble disappeared entirely from mortuary contexts. Bronze ornaments were absent and from all the burials of this phase, and only two bronze arrowheads were found. However, we find that pig's limbs, cattle bones and fish were placed with the dead, often filling pots. The four children were accompanied by an average of 2.5 pots each. Two were buried with spindle whorls, and one with pig's limb bones.

This is the first time in Southeast Asia that the entire sequence of the Bronze Age has been documented from a single site. It is at once apparent that social behaviour expressed in the rituals of death changed dramatically both from the preceding Neolithic, and during the six centuries of the Bronze Age. After a brief initial phase when mortuary behaviour can be seen elaborating and becoming more complex, for a period of about 150–200 years, perhaps accounting for six to eight generations, the central part of Ban Non Wat served as a cemetery for outstandingly wealthy men, women, infants and children. Graves were positioned in grouped rows. This wealth is seen in sharp relief when their mortuary ritual is compared with that of other sites in Thailand. There is no doubt that they represent the missing dynamic of White and Pigott's summary of the situation in 1996: 'a distinct, isolated area exclusively for well-endowed graves' (Figure 4.4). Wealth then fell away dramatically over a further span of at least three centuries.

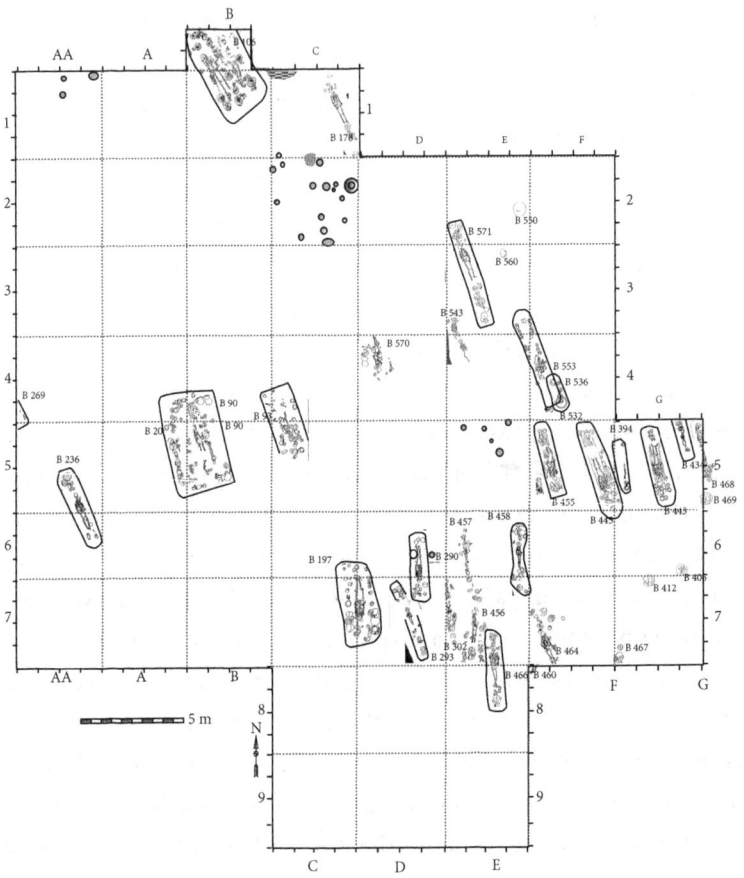

Figure 4.4 The layout of Bronze Age 2 graves at Ban Non Wat.

How can we understand the sharp rise and then fall in how the dead were treated?

Throughout the course of the Bronze Age, the corpse was dressed and wrapped in a shroud wearing personal items of jewellery and interred in a wooden coffin. Pottery vessels were placed in groups, often still with their lids in place. Food was regularly placed in the graves, particularly pig's limb bones but also the remains of cattle, chickens, fish, shellfish and a bird's egg. All the pots found in BA1 graves could have contained food and drink for the deceased. With BA2, food remains included pigs, a chicken, fish and shellfish. The pot forms also suggest possible functions. Small cord-marked vessels were probably food vessels, as are similar forms today. Footed open bowls could have displayed food. Saucer-shaped vessels were found in place as lids. The complexity of BA2 male burial rituals is particularly seen in the large grave containing burials 20 and 90. Burial 90, a mid-adult male, had been placed centrally within the grave, while a younger man's remains were located at the north-western corner. There are 32 vessels described as fine food bowls and a similar number are thought to have contained drink. Both bodies had been partially exhumed not long after burial, and the bones then carefully replaced. This had displaced the ornaments and other offering with the central burial, which was found littered with shell beads, broken shell bangles, as well as a bronze axe and a chisel. Burials 105 and 106 were also found in the same grave, both were women, and one had also been partially exhumed.

How infants were treated in death is particularly revealing because they would not, in their brief lives, have had the opportunity to attain any personal social distinction. Their burial was therefore a statement of how their immediate relatives perceived themselves in society. We find that infants were interred with many ceramic vessels, personal ornaments, at least two copper-base axes, bivalve shells and articulating pig's limb bones. A fine painted design in the form of a stylized human face decorated one vessel. The jars containing infants were also of outstanding quality and contained miniature food and drink vessels.

Although burials of BA3A were laid out on a new orientation, the rituals evident from the layout of the body and the associated offerings are similar. Pig bones are found with the majority of the dead, and one woman was also accompanied by cattle bones. There were typological changes in the forms of some ceramic vessels, others remained identical. Large vessels described as liquid containers were identified usually at the head end of the grave. Small cord-marked food vessels are numerous and often found upright despite their round bases. There are also many decorated drinking vessels and the more elaborate pots of a form that suggests that they contained food. Pots that could have been used to display or receive small quantities of food, or be used as lids to seal vessels once placed in the grave, are also frequently encountered. However with BA3B there was a sharp fall in personal wealth. One or two relatively wealthy individuals were found, but the majority were poor. Some individuals, for example, were accompanied only by two or three pots. The burial rituals of BA4 and 5 as we have seen, continued to be markedly poorer than their predecessors.

A model for social change

The outburst of social display at Ban Non Wat during the early Bronze Age requires a reconsideration of the social impact of metallurgy in Southeast Asia. In doing so, I turn to the political model as described by Hayden (2001a, b, 2009), a model that involves the behaviour of aggrandizer individuals in transegalitarian societies (Clark and Blake 1996). An essential element in such societies is competitive emulation for status, involving differential access to resources and social distinctions based on prestige and wealth. A transegalitarian society may thus be defined as one in which social inequalities are defined and expressed by the private ownership of rare prestige goods, and the accumulation of valuables that can be employed through such a medium as feasting to distinguish the relative wealth and status of different corporate groups within society. Social inequalities, while compatible with some heterarchic features, can be perceived archaeologically through the presence of distinctively large houses, the construction of ritual monuments or facilities and the demonstration of wealth through mortuary indicators, particularly when adults and young are restricted to a specific burial area. Success for a particular lineage within the community turns among other factors, on charismatic leadership, wealth creation, the display of valuables in life and the provision of debt obligations at death by the giving of opulent feasts (Owens and Hayden 1997, Dietler and Hayden 2001).

Clark and Blake (1996) have emphasized the role of aggrandizers in generating social distinctions through their pursuit of prestige and esteem. Their model of transegalitarian social change, formulated in the context of the archaeological record in the Mazatan region of coastal Mexico, incorporates ideas that are directly relevant to the present discussion. It begins with the notion that human societies include aggrandizers, those who seek renown and prestige. How can this be achieved within a single generation, and by what means might it be transferred through succeeding generations? It is certainly advantageous to live in a community that has unfettered access to others of similar standing, in a physical environment where exchange routes employing passes or river routes favour access to prestige valuables. In this respect, the inhabitants of Ban Non Wat could take advantage of the Mun River as a conduit for goods from remote sources. The flat river floodplain is well suited to rice cultivation and there is an abundant supply of salt, still used to preserve wet season fish for dry season consumption. There is then, ample opportunity for aggrandizers to accumulate valuables for competitive display and emulation. Already during the Neolithic, marine shell was being obtained through exchange.

With the Bronze Age, marble, copper and tin were added to the list of valuables that could be used to display social prominence. And this brings one to the core of the issue. As Clark and Blake have written, 'The conversion of external resources into social leverage locally requires (near) exclusive access to outside goods, material or information' (Clark and Blake 1996: 19). When this monopolizing of desirables is maintained, then high esteem and rank can be passed down the generations. However, the system has an inherent fragility. Failure to maintain exclusive access to wealth, and the provision of opulent ceremonials such as mortuary feasting, can negate many years, if not generations, of social endeavour. It is genuinely a case of snakes and ladders.

The issue to be addressed, is whether or not the new data from Ban Non Wat reformulate a heterarchic model by identifying aggrandizers and durable social elites. By following Hayden's (2001a) political model, we can seek signals in the mortuary record for some at least, of the behaviour he identifies as reflecting aggrandizers. It is suggested that the clearest evidence lies in the weight of exotic ornaments worn by the dead during BA2 and 3A. The amount of marine shell and marble jewellery encountered is unprecedented in Southeast Asia. Again, many of these same wealthy individuals were also interred with copper-base axes, chisels, awls, bells and anklets. Given the presence in another part of Ban Non Wat, and at Ban Lum Khao, of contemporary but poor graves, I conclude that there is compelling evidence for preferential access to valuables that reflect status and achievement.

The graves of BA2 and 3A contain the severed limbs of pigs, on occasion fish remains and shellfish. The dead were also interred with many large and elegantly ornamented pottery vessels. Pottery vessels are virtually ubiquitous in Southeast Asian Bronze Age burials, but the number and size of those involved at Ban Non Wat reflect particularly lavish mortuary rituals including opulent feasts. As Hayden (2001b, 2009) has pointed out, the mortuary feasts are a means of demonstrating social prowess, and provisioning them requires the accumulation and deployment of food surpluses that in their turn, establish ties with elites from other communities while at the same time creating reciprocal debts. The degree to which such debts can be repaid is a clear measure of social relativities.

Investment in children is a further avenue whereby aggrandizers can achieve their ambitions. Ceremonial feasting during rites of passage is a means of ensuring successful and profitable affinal relationships. While such activities are beyond archaeological visibility, the treatment of infants, children and the young at death is graphically seen in their graves. One of the most arresting aspects of excavating BA2 and 3A contexts at Ban Non Wat, was to trace the outline of a grave larger than necessary to contain an adult, and find within, the remains of an infant barely a year old accompanied by a copper-base axe, hundreds of shell beads and 20 pottery vessels. All infants during the early Bronze Age were interred with multiple prestige items. The same situation is found with young men and women. It is worth considering for a moment, the labour that would have been necessary for the manufacture of over 23,000 shell disc beads found with one woman, or the 65 trochus shell bangles found with a BA3A man. One man in BA2 was accompanied by three socketed copper-base axes. This wealth is seen as the result of the conversion of surpluses into prestige items.

Aggrandizers, again following Hayden, commonly lay claim to direct communication with influential and revered community ancestors. This might assist our understanding of a singular characteristic of the BA2 cemetery: five adults had been interred with rich and intense rituals, only for their bones to be exhumed at a later date before being placed back in the grave. This was a deliberate and carefully executed social act. Burials 20 and 90 were both men who shared a particularly large grave. Cut marks on the femora of the latter indicate that the body from the knees to the head was taken from the grave without disturbing the surrounding pottery vessels. In the case of burial 20, while part of the body remained undisturbed the head and major limb bones had been removed, again without toppling the adjacent pots, and then neatly replaced with the head on the top of a stack of bones looking eastwards. Such exhumation is restricted to the particularly rich BA2 people. While speculative, it is suggested that this practice might have involved taking ancestral remains to participate in further rituals, thereby exhibiting the aggrandizers' special esoteric power. One of the most compelling images from this period comes from the surface of a pottery vessel in the form of a stemmed fruit bowl. Buried with a wealthy infant, it was decorated with the painted design of a human face. This face with its haunting eyes was embellished with curvilinear designs. Could it be an ancestral figure? (See Figure 4.5.) In terms of the actual layout of the BA2 and 3 cemeteries at Ban Non Wat, the considerable area uncovered has allowed us to trace their boundaries. This reveals beyond any reasonable doubt, a reserved area for a wealthy corporate group or lineage. Again, the reservation of such an area for their own members is a widely identified aspect of aggrandizer lineages.

Figure 4.5 A Bronze Age 2 pottery vessel was painted with the image of an ancestral human face.

The mortuary evidence at Ban Non Wat is extensive and compelling, but the area and internal structure of the settlement remains fugitive and under investigation. Evidence for bronze casting at Ban Non Wat has been identified on the basis of crucibles, moulds and furnaces (Cawte 2007). Over 400 fragmentary moulds, predominantly of clay but also of sandstone, have been identified, as well as 29 complete clay moulds for casting axes and bangles from burial 549 (BA4). Six hundred and sixty-four crucible fragments have also been recovered. Two parts of the excavated area of the site appear to have been employed in casting bronzes, given the local concentration of moulds, crucibles and fragments of bronze. In his exhaustive study of the Ban Non Wat bronze industry, Cawte (2007) has sought evidence for the presence there of either independent specialists, or a workshop in which attached specialists worked under the control of a social elite. This is not straightforward, because over the 500 years involved, there might have been changes in organization not visible due to the nature of the site's stratigraphy. Much of the layers encompassing the Bronze Age were disturbed by mortuary activity, and assigning an assemblage of moulds or crucibles to any given phase of the Bronze Age is not always possible. It is, however, noted that there are fewer moulds and crucibles in the earlier than in the later BA contexts. While one cannot rule out the presence of a bronze workshop maintained under the control of a social elite somewhere on this site, the weight of evidence rather suggests that bronze founders worked independently within a technical tradition replicated at other Northeast Thai sites such as Non Nok Tha and Ban Na Di. Known copper sources are some distance from Ban Non Wat. Present evidence favours exchange in ingots of copper which were then liquefied and cast in the consumer settlements. These ingots might have arrived as the property of an independent and itinerant specialist, whose output during BA1–3A was commandeered by the elite. On the other hand, an elite might have controlled the exchange in exotic items, such as copper, marine shell and marble, and made ingots available to itinerant specialists to produce to their requirements. Finally, there might have been resident specialists who undertook castings at the behest of the elite. There is some early evidence from the detailed analyses being undertaken to order these alternatives in terms of plausibility. Pryce (pers. comm.) has found that the BA2 axes were made from unalloyed copper. However, Cawte (2007), in his study of the crucibles, had concluded that they were used to cast a copper-tin alloy. It is thus possible that the BA2 items were imported ready-made from an exotic source, and bronze founders were present only with BA4, validated by the presence of the bronze founder.

Whichever the case, the first evidence for copper at Ban Non Wat was coincident with the formation of demarcated sets of outstandingly rich burials that endured for at least two centuries. Rituals were complex. The graves were deep and large. They contained wooden coffins containing shrouded corpses covered in exotic valuables: copper-base anklets and bells, bangles and earrings of marine shell and marble as well as thousands of shell disc beads. There are copper-base axes, awls and chisels. Ceramic vessels were embellished with complex, possibly symbolic, painted designs.

The Bayesian analysis of the radiocarbon determinations for Ban Non Wat indicates that the three phases of the early Bronze Age lasted for nearly two centuries (Higham and Higham 2009). Infants born into this lineage were accorded sumptuous burial rituals even when they died at or soon after birth. If they survived to adulthood, it is suggested that they entered a wealthy lineage of high status.

After two centuries, phase 3B of the Bronze Age at Ban Non Wat maintained the same mortuary tenets – the same orientation, placement of pots and wearing of shell and marble ornaments – but became markedly poorer. This sequence involving a period of sudden wealth followed by relative poverty is not unique to Ban Non Wat. A similar situation unfolded at Varna, on the coast of Bulgaria where a small number of high status burials coincided with the initial use of copper and gold (Higham et al. 2008). The richest burial contained a man interred with a golden sceptre and wearing a golden penis sheath. A brief period of ostentatious display was followed by a sharp decline. A detailed consideration of this site has seen 'Varna as a centre of innovation at the beginning of the Late Eneolithic in terms of the massive accumulation of prestige mortuary exotica, with early elite graves creating the momentum for a successful inter-regional social network' (Higham et al. 2008). The authors invoke Childe's (1930) views on the early Bronze Age when suggesting that at Varna there was a period of rapid social change during which 'new status positions were under negotiation'. This was followed, however, by a phase when there was less competition for elite roles and a reduction in the parading of valuables in mortuary rituals.

I suggest that the recurrent evidence for the inclusion of animal bones at Ban Non Wat, taken in conjunction with the careful placement of pottery vessels reflects mortuary feasting. This remains a widespread practice in Southeast Asia to this day, and its implications have been explored by Hayden (2009). His findings provide insight into why this rite of passage is invested with such social importance. Thus, the open display of wealth, the accumulation and giving of food and the immolation of valuables are a measure of social attainment for the sponsoring social group. The act of giving creates debt obligations from those receiving. Lack of reciprocity in the fullness of time means a commensurate loss of prestige and respect. The social linkages created through giving and receiving provide for alliances between elites in contributing communities. They facilitate access to exchange routes for prestige goods, and for restricted social transactions, such as the formation of affinal relationships. Again, the provision of opulent feasts and attendant display requires the accumulation of wealth items, such as special food, marble or marine shell ornaments and copper. Is it coincidental that the appearance of copper-base axes came just as an elite lineage occupied centre stage at Ban Non Wat? I suggest that the novelty, probably the rarity and certainly the desirability of owning and displaying bronzes contributed significantly to the rise of social elites.

It is concluded that during the eleventh century BC, aggrandizers in the upper Mun Valley began actively to seek prestige and status through controlling and deploying exotic materials and knowledge for social advantage. They were interred with a great weight of exotic ornaments. Even some of their infants were accompanied by copper-base axes. Their graves contained splendid decorated ceramic vessels of forms suited to displaying, distributing and consuming food and drink. The severed limbs of pigs were also placed with the dead. Such competitive emulation recalls the provision of ostentatious mortuary feasting described for the Toraja by Volkman (1985).

White and Hamilton (2009) have proposed that this new evidence for Bronze Age social change at Ban Non Wat is relevant only for the immediate area of the upper Mun Valley. This is clearly so, and equally applicable to all other regions of Southeast Asia that were settled during the early phases of the Bronze Age. The occupants of Ban Non Wat enjoyed a highly strategic and well-endowed area. Their immediate environs contained a valued but restricted resource: salt. There was also considerable potential for increasing production of wealth expressed as domestic animals and crops through forest clearance and water control measures. This site also lies along the path of a major natural exchange route. These are precisely the conditions that would provide opportunities for aggrandizers. By contrast, the consumer settlements of Ban Chiang and Non Nok Tha, upon which White (1995) relied when proposing her model of heterarchy, lack the geographic advantages of the Upper Mun region, and Bronze Age burials at both sites were correspondingly impoverished. The contrast between the BA2 and 3A elite and the Bronze Age inhabitants of Ban

Chiang is elegantly illustrated by comparing the quantity of exotic ornaments. There are 772 trochus or tridacna marine shell bangles at the former, and 159,135 shell beads. The corresponding figures at Ban Chiang are 0 and possibly 4.

It must therefore be asked, why did the mortuary rituals at Ban Non Wat become so much the poorer with BA3B? A major objective in modern feasting is to attract allies in the event of a social setback, a lineage disaster according to Hayden. This might result from crop failure, illness and disease, accusations of sorcery or the lack of charismatic individuals to lead. There is no guarantee of social success, and a sudden falling away in social prestige is never far away. Again, Clark and Blake stress that it takes special circumstances for a lineage of aggrandizers to achieve permanency of elite status. A slackening of control over symbols of status, the development of new trade routes, success through charismatic leadership of a rival group, crop failure, all singly or in conjunction, can spell disaster.

It is possible, therefore, that the wealthy lineage during BA2–3A attained an elite status, but then fell from favour with the rise of another, whose cemetery remains to be identified. It is equally possible, that the prestige and wealth of this community as a whole waned under the competitive pressures inherent in BA society. But what, in fact, happened during BA3B–BA5? Wealth displayed in death rituals certainly fell away, but the procedure remained the same: marble and marine shell were still worn by the dead, albeit in reduced quantities. Pottery vessels for food and drink were still placed in the graves. Pigs' limbs accompanied the dead. Despite the presence of a man interred with multiple clay moulds for casting bangles and anklets, bronzes were now vanishingly rare. Towards the end of BA4 and during the course of BA5, marble and shell virtually ceased from use as personal ornaments. We now find clay and spindle whorls being placed with the dead: it seems that weaving cloth was at least one local industry. The degree of ostentatious display declined, but the principles remained the same.

Social organization from the eleventh to the fifth centuries BC in the upper Mun Valley was, it is held, transegalitarian. The eruption of social display and ostentation that took place with the initial Bronze Age reflects social inequalities that gave differential access to the ownership of resources and access to prestige goods. In the nature of transegalitarian societies, social success achieved by aggrandizers was impermanent, and there was no embedded political control from one centre over its contemporaries. However, by recognizing the validity of social inequalities, BA communities in the Mun Valley endowed their IA descendents with the seeds that, to revert to the words of Muhly (1988), were to generate the 'social, political and economic developments that mark the "rise of the state"'.

5

The Iron Age

A turning point

The fifth century BC was a major turning point in the history of Southeast Asia. During the preceding centuries, the dominant external influences came from the north: first rice farmers, then through exchange and the movement of specialists, the ability to cast bronzes. This new change took place when Southeast Asia became increasingly incorporated into a maritime trade network that involved not only China, but also India and even beyond, to the Near East and the Mediterranean world. For millennia, coastal communities in Southeast Asia had been adapted to blue water sailing, and they were no less capable of long distance voyaging than their contemporaries in India and China.

Naturally, communities commanding strategic locations, such as a natural anchorage, would have been best placed to take advantage of the opportunities offered by such a situation. These would have offered access to new exotic goods that could be used to enhance the status of the owner, but also technical skills and new ideas. Such interactions have been widely identified in the recent past as stimuli to significant structural changes in society. One of the clearest examples of this has been documented on the east coast of Africa. During the nineteenth century, there was a marked increase in coastal trading generated by Arab and Swahili merchants. This presented opportunities for the leaders of small independent villages in the hinterland (Alpers 1969). For an alpha male with aggrandizing ambitions, such as Mataka 1 Nyambi (c. 1800–76), there were two ways in which to obtain high status and power. One was to succeed in warfare, the other was to control trade for the new prestige goods which in this case included beads, brass wire, cloth and salt. Exchange is a two-way process, so he sent caravans down to the coast with ivory and slaves, and when they returned, he was able to accumulate valuables, as well as attract followers by distributing them to those loyal to his leadership. Soon his village became a town, and it was necessary to increase agricultural efficiencies through irrigation and opening more land to cultivation. He began as an ambitious member of a village with a population in the order of only 50–60 people, but on his death, he was interred with 30 youths and the same number of girls, as well as opulent offerings of beads, cloth and salt. His successor, Mataka II, who ruled from 1876–85, established the lines of authority and the ideologies associated with the formation of early states. He appointed administrators to supervise coastal trade, concentrated the ownership of guns, assumed ritual prowess through his proximity to exalted ancestors and appointed his close relatives to rule over dependent villages within his polity. By adopting Islam, he benefited from the intangible aura of a new religion.

These are not isolated cases. Ekholm (1977) has described how in Central Africa, chiefly power was secured and consolidated through the ownership and deployment of prestige articles that included copper, salt and shells. These could be distributed in such a way as to attract followers, and exhibit superior wealth and achievement to potential rivals. Goody (1971), again in the context of precolonial West Africa, has stressed how chiefly control over iron, iron workers and superior weaponry, in a word the means of destruction, can paradoxically bring down the peaceful conditions necessary for trade to prosper. Similar processes may be seen in the United States.

Brenner (1988), for example, has described the impact of European settlement in New England in the seventeenth century, on the native Americans. Essentially, the presence of exotic new settlers presented the indigenous peoples with opportunities to acquire a new range of prestige goods, to develop new trading relations, gain access to new forms of weaponry and engage in new forms of economic activity. Traditionally, ownership of *wampum*, sacred white shell beads, was used to project wealth and status. To this could now be added beads of glass, iron weaponry, brass ornaments, European clothing and many other novel and desirable objects. These combined to create stress and instability as the new opportunities were sought by leaders as they competed for elevated status, authority and power. We encounter, in their burial grounds, clear evidence for the deployment of the new status symbols in the rituals of death. Thus, the successful new aggrandizers were interred with large quantities of shell and glass beads, ornamental rings, iron weapons and even boxes to contain trinkets and desirable objects such as keys.

Appreciating how a new exchange network has influenced the affected societies in the recent past allows us to debate the impact of similar circumstances 2,500 years ago in Southeast Asia. As the Bronze Age drew to a close, there were networks of village communities which cultivated rice, maintained domestic animals, hunted and fished. They maintained trading links that brought them copper and tin, marble and marine shell. Some villages specialized in mining copper ore and casting ingots. At Ban Non Wat, many people were interred with spindle whorls, suggesting some specialization in weaving. This site has also provided evidence for the rise of aggrandizers over a period of several generations before burials fell to a lower level of wealth. The point is that the opening of the maritime trade network encountered communities long accustomed to food production, exchange in exotic valuables and a milieu that encouraged the rise of social elites. Why, then, did the Indian and Chinese show any interest in Southeast

Asia? For the former, it was a combination of two objectives. The first was to develop new trading opportunities, including gold. Indeed their name for the area, Suvannaphumi, means the land of gold. But there were also other products in Southeast Asia that attracted their attention, particularly spices such as cinnamon and cloves. Such spices had been imported into Syria and Egypt as early as the second millennium BC. There was also a religious motivation. The Mauryan emperor of India, Ashoka (304–232 BC) became a devout Buddhist, who sent missionaries east and west. The Chinese were also interested in trade missions, although until the late third century BC, they were embroiled in the long period of Warring States. Thereafter, the Qin and Han emperors incorporated large areas of southern China including northern Vietnam, into their Empire. By the early third century AD, China was divided into three kingdoms, and the Wu Emperor, now excluded from the Silk Road that began in northwestern China, sent missions south to seek a southern, maritime Silk Route.

Khao Sam Kaeo

The impact of all these new forces is best seen as a result of recent excavations at the key site of Khao Sam Kaeo. This was effectively a proto-urban centre, located on the bank of the Tha Taphao River, which commands the strategic neck of peninsular Thailand. Here, the riverine route over the narrow land bridge would have encouraged trade links between east and west. The monsoon also has a major impact. For half the year, the prevailing wind comes from the southwest, but for the rest of the year it changes direction by 180°. This would have entailed an enforced wait before return voyages could be contemplated, thereby bringing together Indian visitors in Southeast Asian ports and vice versa. Nor does one need to look far for local resources that would have attracted trade: peninsular Thailand was once a major source of the world's tin, and is a natural transshipment centre for the passage of spices.

The site covers 54 hectares and incorporates 4 flat-topped hills flanking the river, separated by valley floors. Seventeen defensive walls demarcate the hills, and similar walls have been identified in contemporary Indian sites. Occupation deposits found under the wall foundations have been radiocarbon dated from the fourth to the second centuries BC. There is further occupation evidence on the terraces cut on the hillsides themselves, in the form of small walls, pathways and post holes that would once have supported structures.

Stray finds and, unfortunately, looted collections already revealed links between Khao Sam Kaeo with the wider world even before scientific excavations commenced there. There are Dong Son bronze drums from northern Vietnam, fragments of pottery from the Western Han dynasty of China and inscribed seals bearing Indian Sanskrit names in the Brahmi script. Now, after three seasons of excavations, the dramatic changes that took place in the last few centuries BC are being illuminated with material that comes from firm contexts (Bellina 2001, 2002, 2007, Bellina and Silapanth 2006a, b). Khao Sam Kaeo was clearly a hive of industrial activity. In a detailed analysis of the shape and manufacturing techniques of carnelian beads, Bellina has convincingly demonstrated that as with glass, the Thai carnelians are distinguishable from their Indian counterparts (Bellina 2001, 2007). Local elites, she has suggested, had their own preferences and the market satisfied them. The technical demands of carnelian bead manufacture, requiring a long apprenticeship, has led to the proposal that Indian craftspeople established their workshops at the site to satisfy their new patrons.

At least two areas in the site comprised workshops for manufacturing glass ornaments. Hitherto, the discovery of glass in Iron Age Thai sites was seen as evidence for trade with India. But at Khao Sam Kaeo, it is possible that Indian techniques of glass bead and bracelet production were established locally. The sudden establishment of glass working facilities suggests that Indian specialists came to Khao Sam Kaeo. The chemical composition of the glass confirms this point, for there are very few specimens with an Indian signature. Indeed, by examining beads from other sites, it seems that some of the Khao Sam Kaeo production found its way into Vietnamese and other Thai settlements (Lankton et al. 2006).

Khao Sam Kaeo was also a centre for the forging of iron and the casting of bronzes. The iron forges concentrated in particular areas, and much evidence for smithing has been identified. By at least the mid-third century BC, the smiths were fashioning spears, chisels, knives, arrowheads and billhooks. The presence of crucibles also attests to the casting of bronzes, although some of the bronze artefacts could have been obtained through Indian trade, particularly high-tin bowls common in Indian sites. Bronze birds also match Indian examples, while a fragment of a Han Dynasty mirror originated in China.

At Khao Sam Kaeo, Bouvet (2008) has identified Rouletted Ware which, with its fine paste and brilliant surface finish, is particularly well provenanced at the South Indian site of Arikamedu. These may well represent imported ceramic vessels. A second variety closely resembles the Northern Black Polished Ware from Northern India. In this case, however, the actual clay and its temper may be local to Khao Sam Kaeo. As with the glass manufacture, this suggests that actual Indian specialists might have been present at Khao Sam Kaeo and set up their workshops.

This site holds a key position in any consideration of late prehistoric cultural change in Thailand for here the effervescent fusion of local aspirations with widespread trading links has been revealed. A large and vigorous proto-urban centre grew to cover an area of over 50 hectares. New manufacturing industries were established. Foreign specialists brought their skills to bear and their output reached far into the hinterland, where a demand for exotic and prestigious goods was further stimulated.

Ban Don Ta Phet

Khao Sam Kaeo was one of several coastal sites that rose to prominence during the last few centuries BC. Ban Don Ta Phet, by contrast, is an inland site that commanded the strategic Three Pagodas Pass from Central Thailand west to the Bay of Bengal. In contrast to Khao Sam Kaeo, where virtually no burials have been identified, this is a cemetery site containing many graves within which there is an abundance of evidence for the acquisition of exotic valuables, as well as the establishment of a vigorous local iron industry by the fourth century BC. The cemetery was contained within a ditched enclosure, but the acidic soils meant that few bones have survived, and the form of each burial is determined by the layout of mortuary offerings. Those with iron spears are presumed to have contained men, and the graves with spindle whorls are more likely to have been for women (Woods 2002). Some of the dead were interred with considerable wealth. Burial 55 contained 26 pottery vessels, 11 bronzes, 4 iron objects, 9 spindle whorls and 185 glass beads. Burial 46 also included many pots and among the bronzes, some bowls, bangles and a most remarkable bronze figurine of a fighting cock standing on top of its cage. Burial 56 incorporated two bronze vessels, one of which looks remarkably like those cast in northern Vietnam at this period for its style is quite alien to others from Ban Don Ta Phet. There are also 20 pottery vessels, more glass beads, examples in agate and carnelian and 13 iron objects, including digging tools and spearheads. One of the most important finds comes from burial 73 which, apart from a bronze bowl, an anklet and 12 iron implements, also included a carnelian statuette of a leaping lion. The lion was an early means of representing the Buddha before it became acceptable to portray him in human form and its presence beyond any doubt indicates exchange contact with India.

Whereas weapons were forged from iron, bronzes were used for display or for ornaments including bangles, finger rings and bells. The bronze bowls are particularly significant. The alloy contained a very high proportion of tin, which gives a golden colour at the expense of being brittle. They were cast by the lost wax process, and then reduced in thickness on a lathe. Exterior surfaces were then incised with scenes of women with elaborate coiffures and long ear ornaments, a range of animals including elephants and what look like sheep and horses, neither of which is native to Thailand. There are structures which may be houses, flowers and geometric designs. Virtually identical bowls have been found in contemporary sites in India, and they join carnelians and glass as indications of the growing trade across the Bay of Bengal into Southeast Asia (Glover 1996) (Figure 5.1). Even fragments of fabric

Figure 5.1 The beads from Ban Don Ta Phet evidence close contact with Indian manufacturers.

reveal maritime exchange, for the cotton must come from India, while a thread of silk suggests contact with China (Cameron 2008).

Prohear

The lower Mekong River valley and its many tributaries is a further key nodal area for assessing the seminal cultural changes that took place during the Iron Age. Of the many prehistoric settlements, none has furnished more surprises, and more insight into this period, than Prohear. This village is situated 34 km east of the Mekong in southeastern Cambodia. Like virtually all Iron Age sites in this country, its discovery led to frenzied looting by the local villagers, and it is estimated that at least 1,000 human graves have been ransacked for their contents. However, Andreas Reinecke has led a rescue attempt, and opened a 45 m-long trench 2 to 3 m wide under the principal village road, where looters have found it more difficult to gain access to the prehistoric cemetery (Reinecke et al. 2009).

The wealth of the graves is unparalleled for Iron Age Southeast Asia, and necessitate an entirely new consideration of the nature of society then. There are two phases, the first dating within the period 400–150/100 BC, while the second, which incorporates two sub-phases, followed and lasted until about AD 100. The handful of burials from the first phase are found on an east-to-west orientation, and were markedly poorer than their successors, but still contain glass beads as mortuary offerings. A feature of the later burials is the interment of the body with the head to the south, on occasion within a bronze drum, or covered by a bronze bowl. The drums in question are of the Heger 1 form, which concentrate in the Red River valley to the north. These drums would have required outstanding skill on the part of the bronze founder, and have long been seen as symbolic of high status within the communities that owned them. A child was also interred with a large bronze bell placed between the thighs, the form of which finds no parallels in Southeast Asia.

The later burials also contained many glass beads, and fewer beads of carnelian, agate and garnet. However, the most surprising feature is the quantity and range of gold, silver and electrum ornaments. A wealthy woman in burial 4, for example, was interred with a gold wire bracelet, earrings, hair ornaments and finger rings. She also wore a bronze bracelet that incorporated decoration in the form of water buffalo horns, as well as one forged from iron. She may have been a skilled weaver, for spindle whorls were also found in her grave. The golden ornaments recovered from scientific excavations have been augmented by images taken of some in the hands of village looters before being sold. One of the latter was decorated with an incised image of a horse, another with a tiger. But perhaps the most intriguing was a ring from burial 18, which has the image of a man riding a horse. Until these discoveries, horses were unknown in any context in Southeast Asia other than that on a bowl from Ban Don Ta Phet.

One further problem with the site of Prohear is the acidity of the soil, which has destroyed much of the bone and other organic material. However, there is recurrent evidence from teeth and some surviving bone fragments that pig limbs and jaws were placed in graves. Iron we know was locally forged, since the remains of smithing debris have been found at the site. Iron was employed for ornaments, socketed axes, daggers, knives and in one case, a short sword.

Reinecke et al. (2009) have been faced with the demanding need to offer an interpretation of the prehistory of this unique site. In doing so, they have stressed first that there was a significant set of changes between phases 1 and 2. This involved a new burial orientation, new forms of pottery vessels and a greatly enlarged range of mortuary offerings. When reviewing the possible origins or stimuli for these new items, they have identified a similar practice of placing the head within a bronze vessel or drum at the site of Kele in Guizhou Province, southern China. This is not the only intriguing parallel, for at Kele there is also a bronze disc with a central cone like that at burial 47 at Prohear. Kele belongs to the Yelang culture, one of several chiefdoms of southern China which cast buffalo horns in bronze.

Now from the second century BC, these chiefdoms, the most prominent being the Dian of Yunnan, confronted the southern expansion of Han China. The Western Han in due course, converted them through brute force into provinces of their Empire. Reinecke has most plausibly suggested that émigré groups left their homeland in the face of this military threat, and moved south to the safe haven of the lower Mekong Valley. There, they were in a position not only to exploit the gold and silver resources in this region, but also engage in exchange for the bronze drums that they had been accustomed to owning in their homeland. This explanation, like all such new and innovative hypotheses, is open to testing, and one method currently under investigation, is to analyse the isotopes in the surviving human teeth, for these can indicate if an individual came to Prohear from a different environment.

If confirmed by such research, there is a further implication highly relevant to the origins of the civilization of Angkor. The new pottery style found in the phase 2 burials at Prohear is similar to that recovered from the base of the city of Angkor Borei, a site which as we shall see, is directly ancestral to Angkor.

The inland plains

As one proceeds inland, so evidence for the clear impact of maritime trade and possibly the arrival of new settlers to the Mekong Delta region becomes more muted. Phum Snay is another Iron Age settlement where rescue excavations between 2001–3 saved a fragment of information from looting (O'Reilly et al. 2006). This site is located about 75 km northwest of Angkor, and during the first season, nine human burials were revealed, laid out supine and orientated east west. The radiocarbon determinations suggest that they date to the last two centuries BC. In 2003, a further 14 graves were excavated in a different part of the settlement, and these probably belong in the first two centuries AD. The new media for personal ornamentation reached this site, mainly in the form of glass beads, although many villagers were then wearing looted carnelian and agate ornaments. Ivory bangles were found on the wrists of one prehistoric child and an adult and other ornaments were cast from bronze and forged from iron. We find bronze bangles, finger rings and bells, as well as iron bangles and torcs. Iron was also used for swords, daggers, spears and blades. A woman was found interred with spindle whorls, an iron torc, bronze bangles and an extraordinary ceramic epaulette decorated with water buffalo horns fashioned from iron. Here, we can see an echo of the water buffalo cult so evident at Prohear 350 km to the southeast. Mortuary feasting is also indicated by the provision of graves with ceramic vessels, the left fore-limbs of cattle and pigs, and fish. The pots include forms known as Phimai Black, a distinctive lustrous black burnished ware that is particularly distinctive of sites in the Mun Valley, which is further removed from the sea.

The Mun Valley while inland, is strategically positioned between two major river systems. To the west lies the Chao Phraya Valley and to the east, the Mekong. It thus forms a natural conduit for trade and throughout prehistory, as we have seen, it harboured rich and innovative prehistoric communities. It also commands a key resource: salt. There are many reasons why salt is so desirable in Southeast Asia as a whole. The Mun Valley was also to become an integral part of the future Khmer Kingdom, so its Iron Age deserves close scrutiny.

This has been achieved on the basis of excavations over a period of 15 years, at 4 sites. Like so many prehistoric settlements in the Mun catchment, they are all surrounded by broad moats and banks. According to geomorphological fieldwork, these sites were specifically located next to rivers and the engineering works involved creating high banks round the settlement within which water intake from the river was controlled to form moats. We can thus easily calculate the size of each. Noen U-Loke, for example, measured 400 by 260 m and lay within a belt of five moats 200 m wide. Ban Non Wat is circular, with a diameter of 320 m, and Non Ban Jak is 340 by 180 m. The largest in this group of sites is Non Muang Kao, which has a maximum diameter of 650 by 370 m. These and the other moated sites are thick on the ground. There must have been a substantial population increase with the Iron Age. Moreover, they are large enough to be seen as towns rather than small villages characteristic of earlier periods in this region.

The site of Noen U-Loke is a key settlement for appreciating the Iron Age sequence because its four burial phases cover its entire duration. Ban Non Wat is also significant because the transition from the late Bronze Age into the initial Iron Age is seen in an extensive cemetery. As burials accumulated from west to east, so we can pinpoint the first appearance of iron as a mortuary offering. This took place in the late fifth century AD (Higham and Higham 2009). The late Bronze Age burials in question were not by any means wealthy in terms of mortuary offerings. We find that ceramic vessels were placed with the dead, and these often contained fish skeletons. Bronzes were very rare indeed, as were other exotic items. Spindle whorls and lumps of grey clay, however, were regularly placed with the dead, the former being used to create thread and the latter could have been used to dye cloth. It seems that the community was involved in the production of fabric. This habit continued into the Iron Age, but with the first iron bangles, knives, awls and spears, we also find an increase in the quantity of bronze although it was by no means abundant. Three spears, for example, had an iron blade welded onto a bronze socket. There were also plain bangles and in the case of two infants, technically demanding anklets and bangles bearing decoration cast through the lost wax procedure. There were also two thin socketed bladed artefacts of unknown use, but which are precisely matched in moulds from the Khao Wong Prachan Valley in Central Thailand, and an arrowhead. This early Iron Age phase at Ban Non Wat included a handful of individuals wearing glass ear ornaments and carnelian and agate beads. There were thus some new developments from the late Bronze Age, but they were not as dramatic as those that accompanied the early Bronze Age at this site.

There is only a handful of early Iron Age graves at Noen U-Loke, which lies 1.8 km to the west. Two men were found buried alongside each other but in opposite directions. Each lay in a supine position with the hands by the side. Pottery vessels closely matched in form at the corresponding phase at Ban Non Wat contained food remains: complete fish skeletons, pig and turtle bones. The severed foot bones of pigs were placed with each man. One man was accompanied by a large socketed iron spear and an iron hoe. He also wore shell discs probably inserted into distended ear lobes and four tiger's canines bored for suspension round the neck, matching the bear canines found at Phum Snay. The second man wore two similarly bored pig's tusks. An old woman wore two iron bangles on each wrist and a neck ring of iron. Bronze was used for ornaments: bangles and neck rings, as well as for socketed spears. In one intriguing insight into the health of these people, one young man had suffered from leprosy (Tayles and Buckley 2004).

The second phase of the Iron Age falls within the period from 100 BC to AD 200. It is represented by two tightly clustered groups of burials at Noen U-Loke. The earlier group comprised the graves of two men, two women, a child and an infant. They wore the first glass beads to be found at this site, as well as an agate pendant, some beads of shell and bronze finger rings. Two people were interred with complete pig's skeletons. The later and larger group lay just to the south, and in it, we find a number of singular changes, particularly placing the corpse in a grave filled with white, burnt rice husks. The bones, when encountered, were covered in rice. Long, facetted carnelian beads were restricted to this cluster. Other jewellery included strings of glass beads, agate beads and pendants and bronze toe and finger rings. A bronze spiral ornament was found on the head of a young man. It is evident that the inflow of exotic goods increased at this juncture, and the mortuary rituals took on a new dimension of complexity that was to reach its climax in the following phase 3 (Figure 5.2).

The great wealth of the sites of Prohear and Ban Don Ta Phet, measured in exotic mortuary offerings, began to reach the inland Khorat Plateau by the first couple of centuries AD. At Noen U-Loke, burials continued to be laid out in one of four tight clusters on a chequerboard pattern, each it is thought, made up of successive generations of related individuals. We find in each, the graves of men, women, infants and children. This illuminates the relative wealth and standing of each group. Burnt rice was used to cover the body, and some graves still retained a clay lining and cap. Three of the four clusters contained at least one particularly rich individual. Cluster A, for example, involved a woman aged about 25–30 years at death. Her grave was lined and capped with clay, and contained white burnt rice. She was interred wearing a necklace comprising 68 gold and many agate beads. She also wore two agate pendants at the neck. Four splendid, eggshell thin pottery vessels lay beyond the cranium. Her bronze ornaments comprised 2 ear spirals, 38 or more bangles, 64 finger rings and 9 toe rings. She wore a silver finger ring on her left hand and a silver toe ring on the left foot. Over her upper left arm, there lay an iron knife blade bearing the impressions of fabric. A bimetallic (bronze and iron) ring lay under her head. Infants were also interred with considerable wealth. Burial 122, an infant who died when aged between 3–9 months, was found in a rice bed with at least 7 pottery vessels placed round the body. The infant wore an agate pendant at the neck, and 35 bronze bangles.

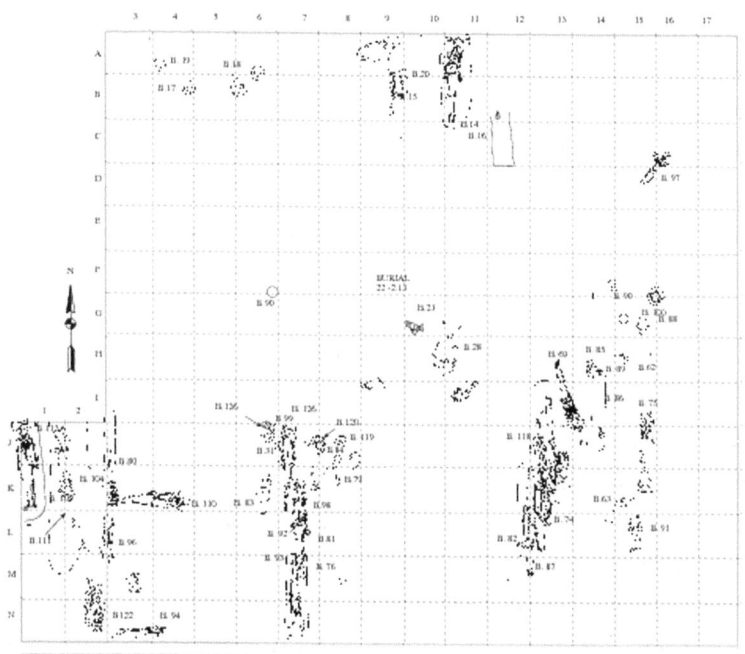

Figure 5.2 Iron Age burials at Noen U-Loke were laid out in clusters and on a grid pattern.

There were also three bangles by the right ear and two by the left, as well as an earring.

Three men, two women and four adults were found in a second cluster, together with the graves of seven infants and a child. One of the men, who died when aged between 25–30 years, was found in a rice-filled grave with 4 pottery vessels. Bronze ornaments were abundant. Two large, circular discs were probably inserted into the ear lobes. He wore four bronze belts, each with a sophisticated form of catch. Nine bronze bangles were present on the left wrist, and at least 11 on the right, while the fingers were covered with over 125 bronze rings and the toes with a further 34 rings. Loose bronze bangles were found beyond the head and over the chest, and four bimetallic rings were recovered, two on the big toe of the left foot, another over the left femur and the fourth under the chin. An iron knife blade had been placed to the right of the head, and an iron arrowhead was present under the leg. By any measure, this man stands out for this great mortuary wealth.

The third cluster incorporated a man who was even richer. This rice-filled grave contained the remains of a male aged 35–40 years at death. At least eight pottery vessels were present. Many glass beads were associated as grave goods. An iron knife was found over the left wrist. Perhaps the most impressive part of the burial, however, was the quantity of bronze. He wore three bronze belts. Seventy-five bangles were present on each arm. There were also 45 finger rings, and at least 2 novel finger spirals on the left hand and 16 rings and 4 spirals on the right. There were also two bronze toe rings on each foot. This man wore two ear coils of silver covered in gold foil. There were also two agate pendants and two bimetallic bronze rings in the area of the neck. The gold covering over silver is a precise match of some of the ornaments recovered from Prohear (Figure 5.3).

An intriguing aspect of this third phase as a whole, is the fact that the last cluster was significantly poorer than the other three. Here, we find a woman whose head had been terribly wounded with a heavy implement. On burial, her head had been placed inside a large pottery vessel. She was accompanied by four spindle whorls. A complete pottery vessel was placed on the left shoulder. Bronze jewellery incorporated four bangles on the left wrist and seven on the right. There were eight key-shaped earrings on each ear, a bronze ring by the neck and another by the left leg. She also wore a single agate neck pendant and a glass bead. There were many infants in thus cluster, but none was interred with the same level of wealth as those in the other three groups.

One of the men during this period was buried with a large, socketed iron spade, reminding us that it was at this time that the banks were thrown up round the site, and a most precious resource given the long dry season, water, was conserved in moats.

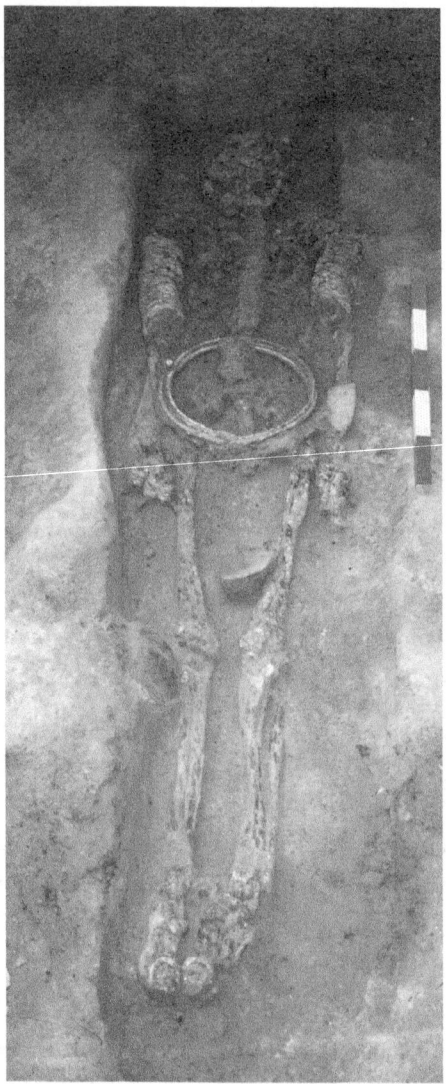

Figure 5.3 Burial 14 at Noen U-Loke involved a man of outstanding wealth, interred wearing 150 bronze bangles, three bronze belts, bronze finger and toe rings and ear ornaments of silver covered with gold.

The final phase at Noen U-Loke saw a clear reduction in the quantity of bronzes and other exotic items placed with the dead, and an end to the tight clustering of burials. Iron sickles were now a regular mortuary offering. Agate and bronzes continued to be worn, but not to the same level of abundance. One young man, intriguingly, had been interred face down, with a sharp arrowhead that had pierced his spinal column. The occupation levels of this phase, which probably lasted from about AD 400–600, also contain many iron points. It seems that conflict was an issue for those living in these large, moated settlements. These sites are also associated with groups of small, steep-sided mounds covered in coarse cord-marked pottery. These on examination, turn out to be centres for extracting salt. The technique continues to this day, as villagers accumulate the salty surface soil, run water through it to create brine, then boil it to leave a thick crust of salt.

These moated sites were clearly then, centres of industrial activity. In addition to the manufacture of salt, the Iron Age populace was engaged in the creation of the yarn needed to weave fabrics. There were iron smiths and bronze founders, potters, cattle herders and those who worked in the rice fields. But where did they actually live? This question has only recently been answered with the excavation of the moated site of Non Ban Jak, just 8 km west of Noen U-Loke. Here, the residential quarter of an Iron Age town has been revealed, complete with thick clay wall foundations, superimposed floors, even a town lane (Figure 5.4). One of the chambers seems to have been used for ritual purposes. It had lip to lip pots placed in each corner, and the graves of an adult, a child and an infant within. The child had its head and feet placed within large pottery vessels, while the adult wore several bronze ornaments.

It is suggested that the social structure within these town sites was compatible with the organization of labour to design and construct the surrounding earthworks, and the likely leaders in this society were quite probably those interred with gold and silver, bronze belts and exotic carnelian, agate and glass jewellery. The production and deployment of salt, coping with conflict and securing exchange relationships all combine to generate social change involving the rise

Figure 5.4 At Non Ban Jak, the residential quarter of an Iron Age town has been uncovered, with a narrow lane and a chamber reserved for burials.

of leaders. We can also trace similar trends in Central Thailand, where the copper mining and processing sites of the Khao Wong Prachan Valley witnessed a surge in output at this juncture. The copper ingot moulds found there could well have fed the output into exchange networks that involved the Mun Valley. Associated burials display just the same indications of a growing wealthy elite: coffins at Nil Kham Haeng contained individuals with multiple iron bangles and pots containing thin cast bronze implements. There are also fine bronze bangles and carnelian beads that mirror precisely those found in coastal sites and in the Mun Valley. Just the same can be said for the Iron Age sites of Tha Kae and Phu Noi.

Any debate on the origins of Southeast Asian civilizations needs to take into account the seminal changes in behaviour that took place during the Iron Age. Many of these were generated with the opening up of a maritime exchange network during the last four centuries BC. This brought a novel suite of trade goods that could be used to project status, centring on glass and hardstone beads. These replaced the traditional use of marine shell and marble. It is important that this procedure involved not just importing the new range, but also the settlement of Indian specialists in Southeast Asian port cities like Khao Sam Kaeo. The new evidence from Prohear has also suggested to Reinecke that the strategic lower Mekong region was settled by immigrants from southern China, who would have been fully familiar with the powerful and expansionary Han state. It is quite possible that knowledge of the properties of iron was also introduced at this time and in virtually all the Iron Age sites examined, there is evidence for the forging of weaponry: there are short swords, daggers, socketed spearheads and arrowheads. Friction and competition were growing in intensity. The human remains of Phum Snay have revealed considerable evidence for bone trauma compatible with hand to hand fighting (Domett et al. 2011) and at Noen U-Loke, a young man had his backbone severed by an iron arrowhead. The excavations in the Mun Valley have revealed the development of veritable towns, each secured within broad moats and banks, within which a wide range of manufacturing activities were centred.

It is therefore possible to integrate a series of factors that would have encouraged a sharp rise in social complexity as well as increased stress caused by competition. These include the introduction of a new range of desirable but exotic valuables control of which would have conferred increased social standing: gold, silver, iron, carnelian, glass and agate. There was the potential to concentrate wealth through the production and exchange of salt, rice, domestic water buffaloes, pigs, cloth and fine ceramics. Competition over valued or scarce resources can be inferred from their selective presence in elite graves. The concentration of sites in the best agricultural land and strategic coastal riverine trade routes likewise would have fostered competition, and increasing conflict would have encouraged investment in leadership. The sequel to these changes will now be examined.

6

The Transition into Early States

The Iron Age was a period of social ferment. Iron ore is much more widespread in nature than copper or tin, and once the techniques for smelting it to produce an iron bloom are understood, iron has transformative properties. This is clearly illustrated by examining how iron was deployed. The dead for example, often wore iron ornaments, particularly bangles and neck rings. At Ban Non Wat, tool kits were placed with the deceased that included knives and awls. Socketed iron spears were forged, as were arrowheads, daggers and short swords. We also find socketed axes, billhooks, sickles, spades and hoes. Iron, in sum, was used in agriculture, warfare, bodily decoration and in engineering as seen in the construction of the banks and moats round settlements. We can also imagine that it was valued for construction in wood: houses, boats and coffins. The origins of iron smelting in Southeast Asia may never be identified, but the coincidence of glass, carnelian and agate beads with the first iron artefacts at Ban Non Wat by the late fifth century BC does suggest that the maritime trade links with India were involved. The same coincidence is noted at Ban Don Ta Phet and Khao Sam Kaeo.

Iron was but one of the new and exotic materials that were disseminating through Southeast Asia as the maritime trade gathered pace. We have seen how centuries of skill in hard stone bead manufacture in India were translated to coastal Southeast Asia. Glass workshops were also established and they surely involved Indian specialists moving east to work under the patronage of emerging Southeast Asian elites. A long tradition of valuing marine shell was displaced in favour of these items as well as gold and silver. Bronze, which had been relatively rare during the Bronze Age itself, was now produced in far greater quantities, and output was dominated by jewellery. One man at Noen U-Loke wore 150 bangles and 3 belts. Other ornaments found at this site included bronze earrings, torcs, anklets, finger and toe rings and bells. This surge in production is nowhere better illustrated than in the extensive and deep accumulation of copper processing debris at the Central Thai sites of Nil Kham Haeng and Non Pa Wai, and the energy expended in the mining of copper at Sepon in Laos.

The growth in the number and size of settlements strongly suggests that the Iron Age witnessed marked population growth, which itself would have stressed the importance of increasing agricultural production. It may well be, given the contemporary rise in the number of domestic water buffalo bones, that these powerful beasts were now yoked to a plough although unlike contemporary sites in northern Vietnam, no ploughshares have been found in Thailand or Cambodia. Certainly, there must have been rice surpluses to be used in mortuary rituals, given the filling of graves with rice at Noen U-Loke and related sites in the upper Mun Valley.

Key issues

There are some key issues to be taken into account when debating the transition from these competitive Iron Age communities into early states. Flannery, for example, has stressed the importance of agency, that is the ambition and charisma of individual leaders to dominate. As he has noted, 'Aggressive human agents are born in all cultures in all epochs' (Flannery 1999). To illustrate test cases of sudden cultural change, he identified five examples of human agency in the rapid development of an early state, from Shaka in Zululand to andrianampoinimerina in Malagasy and Kamehameha in Hawaii. These have led him to suggest a list of instructions on state formation for the would-be aggrandizer: be an alpha male, with aggressive ambitions, be a skilled military commander, and seek competitive advantages over rivals. As your power grows, use corvée labour to increase production, so that you can sustain your followers, delegate authority over newly gained territory to trusted relatives and claim special powers by changing the current ideology. These recommendations reflect the processes listed by Carneiro (1992) for state formation, which involve the defeat of rivals, the taking of slaves, placement of close supporters over conquered territory, the requirement of tribute payments and the maintenance of the forces of destruction, that is, a well-equipped soldiery.

A Chinese mission

To delve into the mechanics of this particular transition in Southeast Asia, it is helpful to view what was going on through the eyes of Kang Dai and Zhu Ying, two Chinese emissaries sent on a mission by the Wu Emperor of southern China in the mid-third century AD. With the end of the Eastern Han Dynasty, China was divided into three kingdoms. The most southerly, known as Wu, was denied access to the riches that could be made by trading along the Silk Road. Hence the Emperor's decision to seek out an alternative, maritime route. We do not know precisely where Kang Dai and Zhu Ying made landfall, but most evidence points to the flat delta lands of the Mekong River. His report, which emerged through its translation into French from the Chinese archives by Paul Pelliot (1903), included the names of a dynasty of rulers of a state they named Funan. They wrote that the founder of a line of rulers was named Kaundinya, an Indian who married a local princess. This, Pelliot suggested, probably took place in the first century AD. His son and further male descendants were placed in charge of defeated and now dependent territories. One of these, named Fan Shih-man, was clearly a man of prowess who mounted maritime expeditions to expand his dominion. Clouded as this might be by time and translation, it still accords with Flannery's identification of the power of the individual and agency. The Chinese visitors also recorded the presence of walled settlements, a palace, and a system of taxation in gold and silver, perfumes and pearls. The local people, they said, used a system of writing using a script of Indian origin, and they encountered a representative there of an Indian King. There were also local lapidaries and jewellers who engraved stones with chisels. Agriculture was well developed and much rice was produced.

Oc Eo and Funan

The publication of this remarkable document in French challenged archaeologists to identify and examine the remains of these settlements, if they ever actually existed. The first clues came from the air, when canals were seen radiating across the western margins of the Mekong Delta (Paris 1929, 1931, 1941). At one nodal point in this canal system, the waterways coincided with the walls and moats round a rectangular site measuring 3.0 by 1.5 km. Excavation at this site, known as Oc Eo, took place in 1944 under the direction of Louis Malleret, and after a long interval, continued in 1998 (Malleret 1959–63, Manguin and Vo Si Khai 2000). Both confirmed the Chinese reports. Impressive foundations for brick buildings, probably temples, reflect Indian building methods. Both through excavations and assembling a collection of artefacts from the local looters, Malleret was able to identify the long reach of the maritime exchange system of which Oc Eo was a part: thus two Roman coins date to the second century AD reigns of Antoninus Pius and Marcus Aurelius. Jewellery came to the site from the Mediterranean, and mirrors from Han China. Iranian coins reached Oc Eo, and some of the rings and seals were inscribed in the Indian Brahmi script dating from the first to the fifth centuries AD. The range of precious or semi-precious stones combined with gold and converted into jewellery in the Oc Eo workshops, is remarkable: diamonds, amethyst, sapphires, rubies, topaz, beryl, onyx, agate, carnelian and quartz.

The labour required to construct the defensive walls, brick buildings and interior canal system at Oc Eo must have been considerable, but beyond this site, even more organization of manpower would have been necessary for the digging and maintenance of the canals system. This flat delta terrain is to this day best traversed by boat, and one of the Funan canals covers a distance of 85 km before reaching a second major centre known today as Angkor Borei. Here, the city walls enclose an area of about 300 ha., while one of the associated reservoirs extends over 20,000 square metres. Miriam Stark has greatly expanded our knowledge of this site through surveys within the walls and across the hinterland (Stark et al. 1999). Her excavations have revealed a long occupation sequence during the course of which deposits over five m deep began with an Iron Age cemetery dating to the third or fourth centuries BC. The subsequent historic period occupation was contemporary with Oc Eo and yielded a similar material culture.

Archaeological research into the Funan phenomenon has accelerated recently, and many more sites are now known. Impressive wooden images of the Buddha have survived in the anaerobic delta mud at Go Thap. At Nen Chua, brick and stone temple foundations as well as a stone linga have been uncovered (Le Xuan Diem et al. 1995). The linga, a phallic object, is a central cult object of Hinduism and was widely adopted as an object of veneration in Southeast Asia. Small brick chambers incorporated into this structure contained cremated human bone and offerings of gold leaf decorated with images representing Shiva and Vishnu, both central Hindu deities. Dating to the fifth and sixth centuries AD, these burials show how Hinduism, associated with the practice of cremation, had taken root in this part of Southeast Asia. The same evidence comes from Go Thap, where a Funan burial site covered a prehistoric settlement. More brick-lined chambers here contained cremated human bone, while offerings included glass and semi-precious stone beads, and gold leaves decorated with Vishnu in his avatar as a turtle. An entire sacred Buddhist text was found impressed into gold at the site of Go Xoai on the delta, dating probably to the seventh or eighth centuries AD.

The names of the line of rulers recorded by Kang Dai and Zhu Ying were probably in an indigenous language. Over the course of time, however, leaders adopted Indian names that denoted high status. We know this, because a handful of inscriptions contain texts which provide important clues as to political events during the later history of Funan. These texts were inscribed on stone stelae in Sanskrit, the priestly language of Hinduism. One of these mentions a king whose name began with Ja.. although part of the text is missing. His full name was probably Jayavarman. Jaya means victory, and varman as a suffix can be translated as protégé of, or protector. This text mentions a prince named Gunavaman, who consecrated a footprint of the Hindu god Vishnu. He was also responsible for reclaiming marshland for productive cultivation. A second text mentions a certain Rudravarman, who was the son of Jayavarman. He appointed an official to inspect royal property. Jayavarman celebrated a military victory in a third text, which also describes how his wife Kulaprabhavati founded a temple. Such meritorious acts were to become commonplace in the ensuing centuries.

These rapid and significant social changes were not confined to the delta. Over 500 km to the north, near the confluence of Mun and the Mekong rivers, there is a mountain with a summit in the form of a linga. It was in the shadow of this sacred place that a man called Devanika established a settlement and raised an inscription during the second half of the fifth century AD (Higham 2004). In it, he described how coming from afar, he claimed the title king of kings after many military victories against his enemies. In celebration, he donated many cattle to his temple foundation. Devanika is a Sanskrit name meaning celestial protector.

It is thus possible to identify structural changes in society that took place in the Mekong Delta region and up river during the first six centuries AD. There is no doubt that the increased pace of trade, facilitated by large ocean going vessels, brought new goods, skills, ideas and people to this nodal region. This was not, as was once thought, a one-way process in which rather simple societies were Indianized into early states. We have seen through the levels of cultural complexity that reigned as early as the Bronze Age, and certainly by the early Iron Age in Southeast Asia, that there was an entrenched procedure whereby ambitious leaders were adept at increasing their social standing through the ownership and deployment of prestige goods. The increased flow of such valuables provided new opportunities for social advancement. The leaders at Khao Sam Kaeo and Oc Eo, for example, were now able to corral and control even foreign craft specialists, and have them produce desirable valuables according to their personal specifications. The early Chinese reports talk of the expansion of territory through conquest, and the placement of kinsmen in charge by named rulers. This, as we have seen from nineteenth-century instances of rapid state formation, is a means of expanding personal power and influence. A third way of achieving exalted status is through promoting a new ideology. This in Southeast Asia, involved both Hinduism and Buddhism. The close linkage between emerging rulers and the former is seen in the new temple structures in which lingas were venerated as symbols of state potency. Impressive new names were taken, new land was brought into production, large brick temples were constructed and stone images of the new gods were carved. Indeed, with the Funan phenomenon, we enter a new world of achievement, and further potential.

Chenla

However, all was not well on the delta, for in the sixth century, new trade routes increasingly avoided Funan. Prosperity declined, and sites were abandoned. Its place was taken by competitive chieftaincies in the interior. Extending from the lower reaches of the Mekong to the Mun Valley, they were rooted in the late Iron Age warlike communities that have been documented through excavations at Phum Snay and Noen U-Loke. As with Funan, the name given to these polities comes from Chinese records, the period between about 550 and 800 AD being known as Chenla. Archaeologically, Chenla is best known by its buildings. From the Mun Valley to the upper delta region, there are numerous small centres containing the remains of one-chambered brick built temples. Some of these still retain the stone linga, which was the object of the rituals enacted. The seventh-century temples at Phum Phon in Surin Province, Thailand, are relatively well preserved, and one can see how access was gained to the interior by a set of steps, and so under a decorated stone lintel to the darkened chamber within. The distribution and the form of these temples were reported on in detail through fieldwork undertaken in particular by Henri Parmentier (1927).

One of the largest and most impressive temple complexes is found just to the east of the Great Lake in Cambodia, at a site known as Ishanapura 'The city of Shiva'. Here, a walled precinct contains three temple complexes. The outer wall was decorated with scenes taken from Hindu epics. Each set of temples inside is defined by its own rectangular walled enclosure, within which lie one central and many

Figure 6.1 Temples at Ishanapura were scenes of the ritual worship of lingas. They were entered by ascending steps leading to a portal embellished with a decorated stone lintel.

subsidiary temples (Figure 6.1). These were built on an impressive scale: the southern complex measured 300 by 270 m. Sunken pools were accessed by steps. More temples were scattered through the central part of the site. These brick temples were decorated with impressive scenes that would once have been covered in stucco and painted. Some reveal images of courtly life, in which one can see the ruler looking out from a palace, surrounded by members of his entourage (Figure 6.2).

Figure 6.2 One of the brick built temples of Ishanapura was decorated with scenes from a royal palace. The walls were once covered in stucco and painted.

A surviving Chinese account of a visit to a Chenla centre, possibly even Ishanapura itself, described a great hall where the king gave audiences every third day. He wore a cap of gold and precious stones, and sat on a wooden throne. Five great officials were present to advise him, backed by many more functionaries and guards. Courtiers and officials touched the ground thrice with their heads during audience, and prostrated themselves before the king before retiring. The king also appointed officials to administer the dependent provinces.

Fortunately, the mute archaeological record, and the impressions set down by a Chinese visitor, are not our only sources for Chenla. The tradition of setting in place inscriptions, particularly when a temple was consecrated, allows us to examine contemporary texts. These inscriptions usually begin in Sanskrit with a eulogy to the ruler in question, now invariably given an impressive Sanskrit name. These gave Cœdès and other epigraphers the chance to reconstruct the dynastic sequences of several Chenla statelets. Many such texts were then followed by further information in old Khmer, the native language of Cambodia, which detail the names and the duties of the ordinary people. These also provide glimpses into their lives, the boundaries of the rice fields, paths, orchards and water reservoirs. One particular series of inscriptions covers the sequence of kings ruling from Ishanapura. The first of these was named Bhavavarman, who was descended from a King Viravarman. A particularly revealing text described him as being the overlord of a dependent place called Indrapura. When he died in 600 AD, he was succeeded by his brother, Mahendravarman – 'protégé of the Great Indra'. Apparently the new ruler, as so often seen in the early formation of states, was involved in expeditions to gain more territory, for there is a set of his inscriptions that record military successes up the valley of the Mun River. It is worth noting that these would have been at about the same time that many of the moated Iron Age settlements there were either still occupied, or soon to be abandoned. The dynasty continued with the accession of Ishanavarman, he who founded some of the major temples at the capital. He too seems to have been a ruler of considerable charisma, for his inscriptions claimed control over dependencies over a large part of lowland Cambodia. He placed his son, for example, as ruler of Jyesthapura, while another magnate at Tamrapura acknowledged himself as a vassal. With Jayavarman 1st (c 635–80), we encounter a ruler of this dynasty who most probably put in place the sort of transformational changes that herald the formation of a state society. His inscriptions, for example, name high officials, such as the President of the Royal Court. There were legal sanctions against those who disobeyed royal edicts. Other officials were officers of the royal guards, chief of the rowers, and chief of the elephants, animals then prominent in the conduct of warfare. Jayavarman also went to war in the autumn, when his enemy's moats were dry. The presence of an official in charge of the royal grain store suggests that by now, rice surpluses were being taxed and conveyed to the centre, in order to sustain the ruler and his followers. These high officials were given honorific titles and symbols, such as the parasol, an item that continued into the Angkorian period to indicate status.

It is the inscriptions rather than archaeological research that illuminate the Chenla period. They make it clear that there was no unified single state, but rather a welter of small polities whose reach and influence rather waxed and waned with the charisma and power of their leader. The temple was a focal point of both religious and economic activities, the recipient of meritorious donations, and the redistribution of surpluses. These were measured in rice, cloth, cattle and water buffaloes and a wide range of other products. We read of male leaders with the title of *pon*, who exercised authority not only over temple transactions, but also the provision and maintenance of water reservoirs and the labour required to bring in the surpluses that were crucial for the maintenance of the upper levels of society. So hereditary classes were forming, ranging from the royal lineage graced with exotic Sanskrit names, a growing body of administrators, military officers and specialist soldiers. The large number of rice field workers, weavers, iron workers, dancers and servants of the temple retained their Khmer names.

Echoes of what we find in the inscriptions can be identified in the later Iron Age settlements excavated in the Mun Valley. The timing overlaps, for where the Chenla period began in about 550 AD, the latest occupation of Noen U-Loke probably extended to the early seventh century. The richly endowed individuals at this site, whose graves incorporated large quantities of rice as well as gold, silver, agate and carnelian ornaments, lived at a time when large water control measures were put in place round settlements in which many of the activities mentioned in the inscriptions were undertaken: iron forging, bronze casting, pottery making and weaving.

For the sequel to the Chenla period of competing polities, some of which were on the brink of if not already states in their own right, it is necessary to turn to an inscription set up in AD 1069 at the Thai temple site of Sdok Kak Thom. It was inscribed following a period of civil strife in the kingdom of Angkor, as noble families were intent on recording their ancestral land rights, and set out the lineage of the local grandee line back to the foundation of Angkor. Sadasiva describes how a ruler named Jayavarman II required his ancestor Sivakavalya and his entire family to follow his move from their base in Southeastern Cambodia on a long journey that ended on the northern shore of the Tonle Sap. The point of origin was probably the large, moated city of Banteay Prei Nokor on the left bank of the Mekong River. Other grandee families tell the same story. This exodus involved much conflict and the taking of new territory. Jayavarman II must have wielded considerable force, and his followers were rewarded with grants of land. He finished this journey in the region that was to become Angkor. This was an adroit choice, for the new capital lay on the northern margins of the Great Lake, or Tonle Sap. This remarkable body of water expands and contracts with the monsoon. As the waters recede, an extensive area opens up for the cultivation of rice. The lake itself provides an inexhaustible supply of fish as well as easy transportation to other parts of Northern Cambodia. It was an inspired choice.

The sequel

We know little of Jayavarman II, and virtually nothing of his successor, who had the same name. However, with the accession of the third king Indravarman, it is possible to identify many of the organizational structures that were to be part of the fabric of this civilization for the ensuing five centuries. In the first place, he was not the direct descendant of Jayavarman IIIrd, but his step-cousin once removed. This reflects the absence of a firm system of male primogeniture, and the succession was often witness to civil war. Thus in one of his inscriptions, it was said that 'his sword fell on his enemies scattering them to all points of the compass'. His capital was then located 15 km southeast of the centre of Angkor itself, the latter location being chosen by his son Yashovarman on his death. Therefore at Hariharalaya, also known as the Roluos group, there survives an early Angkorian centre with few later additions.

One of the most notable constructions was a reservoir, or baray, far larger than anything previously known, but which itself was to be dwarfed by Eastern Baray built by his son. This baray was known as the Indratataka, and measured 3.8 by 0.75 km. Fed by the waters diverted from the Roluos River, its purpose according to a contemporary inscription was to 'mirror his glory, like an ocean'. Until recently, the purpose of these reservoirs was debated. Were they indeed, designed to symbolize the power of the king, or did they have an economic use in feeding water into rice fields. We know now that the two biggest barays at Angkor were both. The Indratataka would certainly have provided the water that reticulated south into the moats that surrounded a series of temples constructed by this third Angkorian king.

The first of these is known today as Preah Ko, meaning sacred bull. Three statues of a bull lie in front of the temple, representing Nandi, the sacred mount of the Hindu god Shiva. This temple was constructed, according to the texts that are found on the entrance ways, to honour and worship the royal ancestors. The three brick shrines in the front of the group were dedicated to Jayavarman IInd, and the king's father and grandfather. The three shrines to the rear honoured their respective wives. Although today the walls are in brick, surviving fragments of stucco reveal the intricate decoration that once would have covered the entire edifice, which was dedicated in the year 879. The foundations texts also demonstrate a tendency that was to last right through to the thirteenth century: such temples were sustained by assigning to them the surpluses produced by village communities. The temples, after all, required maintenance. They were staffed by high priests, and other necessary officials and office holders. They had to be sustained with food and clothing, while the temple paraphernalia included vessels of gold and silver, mirrors with gold supports, libation vessels and perfumes. There was then, a direct link between the royal centre and the communities in the countryside, where workers, tied to their place of birth, were required to work two weeks in four for their masters, and the balance of the month for themselves.

The Bakong temple lies south of Preah Ko. The outer of two moats encloses here, an area of 900 by 700 m. It is entered by means of a bridge across a broad inner moat, flanked by sacred seven-headed naga snakes in stone. Dedicated just two years after Preah Ko in 881, it was built on an unprecedented scale of huge sandstone blocks that were carved with scenes from Hindu epics. A text notes that the central temple, which was replaced by a later structure, contained the state linga named Indresvara, thus linking the name of the king with that of the god Shiva. Again we find subsidiary sanctuaries dedicated to the royal ancestors.

When Jayavarman II was consecrated the Cakravartin, or supreme ruler, in a ceremony that as described in the inscriptions, took place in the Kulen upland north of Angkor, he established a dynasty of rulers that lasted for at least two centuries, to be followed by two further dynasties. Angkor, meaning holy city, is the name given today to the kingdom he founded. Over 600 years, it was the dominant power in Southeast Asia and as we now know through research into its prehistory, its foundations had nothing to do with Alexander the Great or the Romans, but everything to do with the ambitions of the indigenous people interacting with and taking advantage of the new ideas, technologies and exotic goods generated with the rise of international exchange along the southern Silk Road.

Bibliography

Alpers, E. A. (1969) 'Trade and society among the Yao in the nineteenth century', *Journal of African History* 93: 405–20.

Ashmore, P. J. (1999) 'Radiocarbon dating: avoiding errors by avoiding mixed samples', *Antiquity* 73: 124–30.

Bayard, D. T. (1980) 'The roots of Indochinese civilization: recent developments in the prehistory of Southeast Asia', *Pacific Affairs* 53: 89–114.

Bellina, B. (2001) *'Témoignages archéologiques d'échanges entre l'Inde et l'Asie du Sud-Est, morphologie, morphométrie et techniques de fabrication des perles en agate et en cornaline (VIe siècle avant notre ère – VIe siècle de notre ère)'*, Mémoires de DEA, Université Sorbonne-Nouvelle, Paris III.

— (2002) 'Le port protohistorique de Khao Sam Kaeo en Thaïlande péninsulaire: lieu privilégié pour l'étude des premières interactions indiennes et sud-est asiatiques', Chroniques, *Bulletin de l'Ecole Française d'Extrême-Orient* 89: 329–43.

— (2007) *Cultural Exchange between India and Southeast Asia. Production and Distribution of Hard Stone Ornaments (VI c. BC– VI c. AD*, Paris: Editions de la Maison des Sciences de l'Homme, with the participation of l'Ecole Française d'Extrême-Orient and Epistèmes.

Bellina, B. and Silapanth, P. (2006a) 'Khao Sam Kaeo and the upper Thai peninsula: understanding the mechanisms of early trans-Asiatic trade and cultural exchange', in E. A. Bacus, I. C. Glover and V. C. Pigott (eds), *Uncovering Southeast Asia's Past*, Singapore, NUS Press: 379–92.

— (2006b) 'Weaving cultural identities on trans-Asiatic networks: Upper Thai-Malay peninsula – an early socio-political landscape', in B. Bellina-Pryce (ed.), The archaeology of prehistoric trans-Asiatic exchange: technological and settlement evidence from Khao Sam Kaeo, *Bulletin de l'Ecole Française d'Extrême-Orient* 93: 257–93.

Bellwood, P., Oxenham, M., Bui Chi Hoang, Nguyen Thi Kim Dung, Willis, A., Sarjeant, C., Piper, P. J., Matsumura, H., Tanaka, K., Beavan, N., Higham, T., Nguyen Quoc, Manh, Dang Ngoc Kinh, Nguyen

Khanh Trung Kien, Vo Thanh Huong, Van Ngoc Bich, Tran Thi Kim Quy, Nguyen Phuong Thao, Campos, F., Sato, Y. I., Nguyen Lan Cuong and Amano, N. In review. 'An Son and the Neolithic of Southern Vietnam'. *Asian Perspectives.*

Bentley, A., Tayles, N. G., Higham, C. F. W., Macpherson, C. and Atkinson, T. C. (2007) 'Shifting gender relations at Khok Phanom Di, Thailand: isotopic evidence from the skeletons', *Current Anthropology* 48(2): 301–14.

Berstan, R., Stott, A. W., Minnit, S., Bronk Ramsey, C., Hedges, R. E. M. and Evershed, R. P. (2008) 'Direct dating of pottery from its organic residues: new precision using compound-specific carbon isotopes', *Antiquity* 82: 702–13.

Boer-Mah, T. (2011) 'The adze assemblage', in C. F. W. Higham and A. Kijngam (eds), *The Origins of the Civilization of Angkor.* Volume IV. *The Excavation Ban Non Wat: The Neolithic Occupation*, Bangkok, The Fine Arts Department of Thailand: 136–68.

Bonsall, C., Cook, G., Manson, J. and Anderson, D. (2002) 'Direct dating of Neolithic pottery: progress and prospects', *Documenta Praehistorica* 29: 47–59.

Bouvet, P. (2006) 'Étude préliminaire de céramique Indienne et "Indienisantes" du site de Khao Sam Kaeo IVe-IIe siècles av. J.-C', in B. Bellina-Pryce (ed.), The archaeology of prehistoric trans-Asiatic exchange: technological and settlement evidence from Khao Sam Kaeo. *Bulletin de l'Ecole Française d'Extrême-Orient* 93: 353–90.

Brenner, E. (1988) 'Sociopolitical implications of mortuary ritual remains in seventeenth century native southern New England', in M. Leone and P. Potter (eds), *The Recovery of Meaning: Historical Archaeology in the Eastern United States.* Washington, Smithsonian Institution: 147–81.

Cameron, J. (2008) 'The archaeological textiles from Ban Don Ta Phet', Paper read at the 12th conference of the European Association of Southeast Asian Archaeologists, Leiden September 2008.

Carneiro, R. L. (1992) 'Point counterpoint. Ecology and ideology in the development of New World civilizations', in A. A. Demarest and G. W. Conrad (eds), *Ideology and Pre-Columbian Civilizations.* Santa Fe, School of American Research Press.

Cawte, H. (2007) 'Smith and society in Bronze Age Thailand', PhD dissertation, University of Otago.

Childe, V. G. (1930) *The Bronze Age*, Cambridge, Cambridge University Press.

Ciarla, R. (2007) 'Rethinking Yuanlongpo: the case for technological links between the Lingnan (PRC) and central Thailand in the Bronze Age', *East and West* 57(1–4): 305–28.

Clark, J. E. and Blake, M. (1996) 'The power of prestige: competitive generosity and the emergence of rank societies in lowland Mesoamerica', in E. M. Brumfiel and J. W. Fox (eds), *Factional Competition and Political Development in the New World*, Cambridge, Cambridge University Press: 17–30.

Cœdès, G. (1968) *The Indianised States of Southeast Asia*, Honolulu, East-West Centre Press.

Colani, M. (1927) 'L'Âge de la pierre dans la province de Hoa Binh', *Mémoires du Service Géologique de l'Indochine* XIII: 1.

Dietler, M. and Hayden, B. (2001) *Feasts: Archaeological and Ethnographic Perspectives on Food, Politics and Power*, Washington, Smithsonian Institution.

Dodo, Y. (2010) 'Qualitative cranio-morphology at Man Bac', in M. Oxenham, H. Matsumura and D. K. Nguyen (eds), *Man Bac. The Excavation of a Neolithic Site in Northern Vietnam. The Biology.* Canberra, Terra Australis 33: 33–42.

Domett, K. M., O'Reilly, D. J. W. and Buckley, H. (2011) 'Biological evidence for conflict in Iron Age Northwest Cambodia', *Antiquity* 85: 441–58.

Ekholm, K. (1977) 'External exchange and the transformation of central African social systems', in J. Friedman and M. J. Rowlands (eds), *The Evolution of Social Systems*, London, Duckworth: 115–36.

Flannery, K. (1999) 'Process and agency in early state formation', *Cambridge Archaeological Journal* 9(1): 3–21.

Foucher, A. (1922) 'L'Art Gréco-bouddique de Gandhara. Étude sur les Origines de L'Influence Classique dans l'Art Bouddique de l'Inde et de l'Extrême Orient', Paris.

Fuller, D. Q., Sato, I., Castillo, C., Qin, L., Weisskopf, A. R., Kingwell-Banham, E. J., Song, J., Ahn, S.-M. and van Etten, J. (2010) 'Consilience of genetics and archaeobotany in the entangled history of rice', *Archaeological and Anthropological Science* 2, 115–31.

Glover, I. C. (1996) 'The southern Silk Road: archaeological evidence for early trade between India and Southeast Asia', in A. Srisuchat (ed.), *Ancient Trades and Cultural Contacts in Southeast Asia*, Bangkok, National Culture Commission: 57–94.

Glusker, D. and White, J. (1997) 'Comment', *Archaeometry* 39: 259–60.

Goody, J. (1971) *Technology, Tradition and the State in Africa*, Hutchinson, London.

Gorman, C. F. and Charoenwongsa, P. (1976) 'Ban Chiang: a mosaic of impressions from the first two years', *Expedition* 8(4): 14–26.

Groslier, B.-P. (2005) *Angkor and Cambodia in the Sixteenth Century: According to Portuguese and Spanish Sources*, Bangkok, Orchid Press.

Ha Van Tan (1997) 'The Hoabinhian and before', *Bulletin of the Indo-Pacific Prehistory Association* 16: 35–41.

Hayden, B. (2001a) 'Richman, poorman, beggarman, chief: the dynamics of social inequality', in G. M. Feinman and T. D. Price (eds), *Archaeology at the Millennium. A Sourcebook*, New York, Kluwer Academic/Plenum: 231–66.

— (2001b) 'The dynamics of wealth and poverty in the transegalitarian societies of Southeast Asia', *Antiquity* 75: 571–81.

— (2009) 'Funeral feasts: why are they so important', *Cambridge Archaeology Journal* 19(1): 29–52.

He, A. and Chen, X. (2008) 'New discovery from the excavation of Chongtang site in Chongzuo, Guangxi', *China Cultural Relics News*: 1621.

Hedges, R. E. M., Tiemei, C. and Housley, R. A. (1992) 'Results and methods in the radiocarbon dating of pottery', *Radiocarbon* 34(3): 906–15.

Higham, C. F. W. (1983) 'The Ban Chiang culture in wider perspective', *Proceedings of the British Academy* LXIX: 229–61.

— (1989) *The Archaeology of Mainland Southeast Asia*, Cambridge, Cambridge University Press.

— (1996) *The Bronze Age of Southeast Asia*, Cambridge, Cambridge University Press.

— (2001) *The Civilization of Angkor*, London, Weidenfeld and Nicolson.

— (2004) 'Before Devanika. Social change and state formation in the Mekong Valley', in J. Cherry, C. Scarre and S. Shennan (eds), *Explaining*

Social Change. Studies in Honour of Colin Renfrew, Cambridge, the McDonald Institute: 203–14.

— (2008) 'Recasting Thailand. New discoveries at Ban Non Wat', *Current World Archaeology* 31: 38–41.

— (2011) 'The Bronze Age of Southeast Asia: new insight on social change from Ban Non Wat', *Cambridge Archaeological Journal* 21(3): 365–89.

Higham, C. F. W. and Higham, T. F. G. (2009) 'A new chronological framework for prehistoric Southeast Asia, based on a Bayesian model from Ban Non Wat', *Antiquity* 82: 1–20.

Higham, C. F. W. and Thosarat, R. (eds) (1998) *The Excavation of Nong Nor, a Prehistoric Site in Central Thailand*, Oxbow Books, Oxford and University of Otago Studies in Prehistoric Anthropology no. 18.

— (2004) *The Excavation of Khok Phanom Di: Volume VII. Summary and Conclusions*, London, The Society of Antiquaries of London.

Higham, C. F. W. and Wiriyaromp, W. (2011) 'Neolithic 1 ceramic motifs', in C. F. W. Higham and A. Kijngam (eds), *The Origins of the Civilization of Angkor. Volume IV. The Excavation Ban Non Wat: The Neolithic Occupation*, Bangkok, The Fine Arts Department of Thailand: 93–106.

Higham, C. F. W., Ciarla, R., Higham, T. F. G., Kijngam, A. and Rispoli, F. (2011) 'The establishment of the Bronze Age in Southeast Asia', *Journal of World Prehistory* 24(4): 227–74.

Higham, T. F. G. (1993) 'The shell knives', in C. F. W. Higham and R. Thosarat (eds), *The Excavation of Khok Phanom Di. Volume 3 (part 1): The Material Culture*. Society of Antiquaries of London, Research Report no. L, London: 177–212.

Higham, T. F. G., Chapman, J., Slavchev, J., Gaydarska, B., Honch, N., Yordanov, Y. and Dimitrova, B. (2008) 'New AMS radiocarbon dates for the Varna Eneolithic Cemetery, Bulgarian Black Sea Coast', *Acta Musei Varnaensis* VI: 95–114.

Hill, C., Soares, P., Mormina, M., Macaulay, V., Meehan, W., Blackburn, J., Clarke, D., Maripa Raja, J., Ismail, P., Bulbeck, D., Oppenheimer, S. and Richards, R. (2006) 'Phylogeography and ethnogenesis of Aboriginal Southeast Asians', *Molecular Biology and Evolution* 12: 2480–91.

Ho, C. M. (1984) *The Pottery of Kok Charoen and its Farther Context*, PhD dissertation, University of London.

Huffer, D. G. and Trinh Hoang Hiep (2010) 'Man Bac burial descriptions', in M. Oxenham, H. Matsumura and D. K. Nguyen (eds), *Man Bac. The Excavation of a Neolithic Site in Northern Vietnam. The Biology,* Canberra, Terra Australis 33: 135–68.

Lankton, J. W., Dussubieux, L. and Gratuze, B. (2006) 'Glass from Khao Sam Kaeo: transferred technology from an early Southeast Asian exchange network', in B. Bellina-Pryce (ed.), The archaeology of prehistoric trans-Asiatic exchange: technological and settlement evidence from Khao Sam Kaeo. *Bulletin de l'Ecole Française d'Extrême-Orient* 93: 317–51.

Le Xuan Diem, Dao Linh Con and Vo Si Khai (1995) *Van Hoa Oc Eo Nhung Kham Pha Moi,* Hanoi, Nha Xuat Ban Khoa Hoc Xa Hoi.

Loofs-Wissowa, H. H. E. (1983) 'The development and spread of metallurgy in Southeast Asia: a review of the present evidence', *Journal of Southeast Asian Studies* 14(1): 1–11, 26–31.

Loubère, S. de la (1693) *A New Historical Relation of the Kingdom of Siam,* London, Thomas Horne.

Majumdar, R. (1944) *Hindu Colonies in the Far East,* Calcutta, General Printers and Publishers.

Malleret, L. (1959–63) *L'Archaeologie du Delta du Mekong,* Paris, Publications de l'École Française d'Extrême-Orient.

Manguin, P.-Y. and Vo Si Khai (2000) 'Excavations at the Ba The/Oc Eo complex (Viet Nam). A preliminary report on the 1998 campaign', in W. Lobo and S. Reimann (eds), *Southeast Asian Archaeology 1998,* Centre for South-East Asian Studies, University of Hull and Ethnologisches Museum, Staatliche Museum zu Berlin: 107–21.

Mansuy, H. (1902) *Stations préhistoriques de Samrong-Sen et de Longprao (Cambodge),* Hanoi, F.H. Scheider.

Matsumura, H. (2010a) 'Quantitative cranio-morphology at Man Bac', in M. Oxenham, H. Matsumura and D. K. Nguyen (eds), *Man Bac. The Excavation of a Neolithic Site in Northern Vietnam. The Biology,* Canberra, Terra Australis 33: 21–32.

— (2010b) 'Quantitative and qualitative dental-morphology at Man Bac', in M. Oxenham, H. Matsumura and D. K. Nguyen (eds), *Man Bac. The Excavation of a Neolithic Site in Northern Vietnam. The Biology,* Canberra, Terra Australis 33: 43–63.

Mormina, M. and Higham, C. F. W. (2010) 'Climate and the population history of Southeast Asia', in A. B. Mainwaring, R. Giegengack and C. Vita-Finzi (eds), *Climate Crises and Human History*, Philadelphia, American Philosophical Society: 197–212.

Muhly, J. (1988) 'The beginnings of metallurgy in the Old World', in R. Maddin (ed.), *The Beginnings of the Use of Metals and Alloys*, Cambridge, MA, MIT Press: 2–20.

Oota, H., Kurosaki, K., Pookajorn, S., Ishida, T. and Ueda, S. (2001) 'Genetic study of the Paleolithic and Neolithic Southeast Asians', *Human Biology* 73: 225–31.

O'Reilly, D. J. W. (2003) 'Further evidence for heterarchy in Bronze Age Thailand', *Asian Perspectives* 44: 300–6.

O'Reilly, D. J. W. von den Driesch, A. and Voeun, V. (2006) 'Archaeology and archaeozoology of Phum Snay: a late prehistoric cemetery in Northwestern Cambodia', *Asian Perspectives* 45 (2): 189–211.

Owens, D. A. and Hayden, B. (1997) 'Prehistoric rites of passage: a comparative study of transegalitarian hunter-gatherers', *Journal of Anthropological Archaeology* 16, 121–61.

Oxenham, M., Matsumura, H. and Nguyen, D. K. (eds) (2010) *Man Bac. The Excavation of a Neolithic Site in Northern Vietnam. The Biology*, Canberra: Terra Australis 33.

Paris, P. (1929) 'Anciens canaux reconnus sur photographies aériennes dans les provinces de Ta-Keo, Chao-Doc, Long-Xuyen et Rach-Gia', *Bulletin de l'Ecole Française d'Extrême-Orient* 29: 365–70.

— (1931) 'Anciens canaux reconnus sur photographies aériennes dans les provinces de Ta-Kev et De Chau-Doc', *Bulletin de l'Ecole Française d'Extrême-Orient* 31: 221–4.

— (1941) 'Notes et melanges: anciens canaux reconnus sur photographies aériennes dans les provinces de Takeo, Chau-Doc, Long-Xuyen et Rach-Gia', *Bulletin de l'Ecole Française d'Extrême-Orient* 41: 365–70.

Parmentier, M. H. (1927) *L'Art Khmer Primitif*, Paris, Publications de l'Ecole Française d'Extrême-Orient XXI–XXII.

Pelliot, P. (1903) 'Le Fou-Nan', *Bulletin de l'Ecole Française d'Extrême-Orient* 2: 248–333.

Pigott, V. C. and Ciarla, R. (2007) 'On the origins of metallurgy in prehistoric Southeast Asia: the view from Thailand', in S. La Niece, D. Hook and P. Craddock (eds), *Metals and Mines: Studies in Archaeometallurgy,* London, Archetype Press in association with the British Museum: 76–88.

Piper, P. J., Campos, F. Z., Ngoc Kinh, D., Amano, N., Oxenham, M., Chi Hoang, B., Bellwood, P. and Willis, A. (2012) 'Early evidence for pig and dog husbandry from the Neolithic site of An Son, Southern Vietnam', *International Journal of Osteoarchaeology,* published on line.

Reinecke, A., Vin Laychour and Seng Sonetra (2009) *The First Golden Age of Cambodia: Excavations at Prohear,* Bonn, German Foreign Office.

Ribadeneyra, F. M. de (1601) *Historia de Las Islas del Archipielago y Reynos de la Grand China,* Barcelona, G. Graells.

Rispoli, F. (2008) 'The incised and impressed pottery style of mainland Southeast Asia: following the paths of Neolithization', *East & West* 57(1–4): 235–304.

Roberts, B. W., Thornton, C. P. and Pigott, V. C. (2009) 'Development of metallurgy in Eurasia', *Antiquity* 83: 1012–22.

Sedov, L. A. (1978) 'Angkor, society and state', in H. J. M. Claesson and P. Skalnik (eds), *The Early State,* The Hague, Mouton: 111–30.

Shinoda, K. (2010) 'Mitochondrial DNA of human remains at Man Bac', in M. Oxenham, H. Matsumura and D. K. Nguyen (eds), *Man Bac. The Excavation of a Neolithic Site in Northern Vietnam. The Biology,* Canberra, Terra Australis 33: 95–116.

Solheim, W. G. II (1968) 'Early bronze in Northeastern Thailand', *Current Anthropology* 9(1): 59–62.

— (1972) 'An earlier agricultural revolution', *Scientific American* CCVI(4): 34–41.

Sørensen, P. (1963) 'North-south indications of a prehistoric migration into Thailand', *East and West* 14: 211–17.

Sørensen, P. and Hatting, T. (1967) *Archaeological Investigations in Thailand.* Volume II, *Ban Kao, Part 1: The Archaeological Materials from the Burials,* Copenhagen, Munksgaard.

Stark, M. T., Griffin, P. B., Chuch Phoeurn, Ledgerwood, J., Dega, M., Mortland, C., Dowling, N., Bayman, J. M., Bong Sovath, Tea Van, Chhan Chamroen and Latinis, K. (1999) 'Results of the 1995–6 archaeological field investigations at Angkor Borei, Cambodia', *Asian Perspectives* 38(1): 7–36.

Tayles, N. G. (1999) *The Excavation of Khok Phanom Di. A Prehistoric Site in Central Thailand.* Volume V: *The People*, Research Reports of the Society of Antiquaries of London No. LXI, London, Society of Antiquaries.

Tayles, N. G. and Buckley, H. R. (2004) 'Leprosy and tuberculosis in Iron Age Southeast Asia?', *American Journal of Physical Anthropology* 125: 239–56.

Thompson, G. B. (1996) *The Excavation of Khok Phanom Di. A Prehistoric Site in Central Thailand.* Volume IV. *Subsistence and Environment: The Botanical Evidence (The Biological Remains, Part II)*, London, Society of Antiquaries of London Research Report LIII.

Vickery, M. (1998) *Society, Economics and Politics in Pre-Angkor Cambodia*, Tokyo, The Centre for East Asian Cultural Studies for Unesco.

Vincent, B. A. (2004) *The Pottery*, London, Research Report of the Society of Antiquaries of London LXX.

Volkman, T. A. (1985) 'Feasts of honor: ritual and change in the Toraja Highlands', *Illinois Studies in Anthropology* No. 16.

Weber, S., Lehman, H., Barela, T., Hawks, S. and Harriman, D. (2010) 'Rice or millets? Early farming strategies in prehistoric central Thailand', *Anthropological and Archaeological Science* 2: 79–88.

White, J. C. (1982) *Ban Chiang. The Discovery of a Lost Bronze Age*, Philadelphia, University of Pennsylvania Press.

— (1995) 'Incorporating heterarchy into theory on socio-political development: the case from Southeast Asia', in R. Ehrenreich, C. Crumley and J. Levy (eds), *Heterarchy and the Analysis of Complex Societies*. Washington, DC, American Anthropological Association: 101–23.

— (1997) 'A brief note on new dates for the Ban Chiang cultural tradition', *Bulletin of the Indo-Pacific Prehistory Association* 16: 103–6.

— (2008) 'Dating early bronze at Ban Chiang, Thailand', in J.-P. Pautreau, A.-S. Coupey, V. Zeitoun and E. Rambault (eds), *From* Homo erectus *To the Living Traditions.* Bougon, European Association of Southeast Asian Archaeologists: 91–110.

White, J. C. and Hamilton, E. (2009) 'The transmission of early Bronze Age technology to Thailand: new perspectives', *Journal of World Prehistory* 22: 357–97.

White, J. C. and Pigott, V. (1996) 'From community craft to regional specialisation: intensification of copper production in pre-state Thailand', in B. Wailes (ed.), *Craft Specialisation and Social Evolution: In Memory of V. Gordon Childe*. University Museum Monograph 93. Philadelphia, University Museum Publications: 151–75.

Woods, M. (2002) 'A spatial and statistical analysis of Ban Don Ta Phet', MA dissertation, School of African and Oriental Studies.

Xie, G. M., Lin, Q. and Peng, C. L. (2003) 'Gexinqiao Neolithic site in Baise City, Guangxi', *Archaeology* 12: 3–6.

Zhang, C. and Hung, H.-C. (2010) 'The emergence of agriculture in southern China', *Antiquity* 84: 11–25.

Index

·